Introduction to Philosophy
&
Ethics

Phil Fernandes
Institute of Biblical Defense

Introduction to Philosophy

Instructor: Dr. Phil Fernandes

Institute of Biblical Defense
P. O. Box 3264
Bremerton, WA. 98310
(360) 698-7382

www.biblicaldefense.org   ibd@sinclair.net

Introduction to Philosophy
Course Overview

1) Introduction to Philosophy (a survey of the discipline of philosophy)

2) Epistemology (what is knowledge?)

3) Metaphysics (what is reality?)

4) Philosophy of Religion (What is the Ultimate?)

5) Ethics (What is good or right?)

Textbook: *Introduction to Philosophy, A Christian Perspective* (by Norman Geisler & Paul Feinberg; Baker Book House)

***the lectures follow the basic structure of the textbook

Part One—Introduction to Philosophy

1) <u>What is Philosophy?</u> (chapter 1)
    A) everyone is a philosopher
    B) 2 Greek words (philos = love; sophia = wisdom)
    C) philosophy is the love of wisdom
    D) Socrates—"the unexamined life is not worth living."
    E) 2 different approaches to philosophy
        1) <u>analytic philosophy</u>—conceptual analysis; the analytic study of concepts
            a) verification principle (truth is definitional or only found through five senses) self-refuting
            b) don't overemphasize defining terms
            c) we need to test the truth of statements as well
        2) <u>speculative philosophy</u>
            a) goes beyond a mere description of the world
            b) speculates how the world should be
    F) <u>definition of philosophy</u> (page 17, Geisler & Feinberg)
        1) the critical analysis of fundamental concepts of human inquiry
        2) the normative discussion of how human thought & action ought to function
        3) the description of the nature of reality
    G) <u>characteristics of philosophical inquiry</u>
        1) disputes usually caused not by facts, but by differing interpretations of facts
        2) often method is more important than theoretical content
        3) one of philosophy's chief goals is clarification
        4) critically examines justification & evidence
        5) focuses on search for truth & important issues discussed by thoughtful men throughout history
        6) analysis & explanation involves appeals to systems of principles
        7) sometimes it deals with the nature of being or reality
    H) <u>the value of philosophy</u>
        1) it can help us to understand society
        2) it can help us overcome prejudice & faulty reasoning
        3) helps us apply biblical/moral principles in gray areas
        4) it can help us refute objections to the gospel
        5) it can help us to understand God & His creation
            (all truth is God's truth)

2) <u>Disciplines Within Philosophy</u> (chapter 2)
- A) <u>Ethics</u> (deals with issues of morality)
- B) <u>Social & Political Philosophy</u> (deals with actions of a group)
- C) <u>Aesthetics</u> (deals with beauty, taste, & art)
- D) <u>Logic</u> (the systematic laws of thought & argument)
    1) law of identity (A = A)
    2) law of noncontradiction (A $\neq$ non-A)
    3) law of causality (non-being cannot cause being)
    4) law of excluded middle (either A or non-A)
    5) law of finality (every agent acts toward an end)
- E) <u>Philosophy of Religion</u>
    1) not history of religions, not comparative religions, not theology
    2) attempts to answer the following questions:
        a) what is religion?
        b) are arguments for God's existence valid?
        c) what are God's attributes? are they compatible?
        d) is religious language possible?
        e) the problem of evil
- F) <u>History of Philosophy</u> (the history of philosophical thought)
- G) <u>Philosophy of History</u> (analyzes the discipline of historical research, it attempts to interpret history, is history linear or cyclical?)
- H) <u>Philosophy of Science</u> (critical examination of scientific concepts & methods)
- I) <u>Philosophy of Law, Mathematics, Education, etc.</u>
- J) <u>Epistemology</u> (looks into the origin & nature of knowledge)
- K) <u>Metaphysics</u> (the study of being or reality; beyond the physical)
- L) <u>Philosophy of Mind</u> (studies the relationship between the body & the mind)
- M) <u>Action Theory</u> (the relationship of mental states to actions)

3) <u>Methodology in Philosophy</u> (chapter 3) methods of seeking truth

    A) <u>Ancient Methods</u>

        1) <u>Socrates' method of interrogation</u> (469-399BC)

            a) the question & answer method

            b) he believed we knew the answers in previous existence (reincarnation)

            c) questioning will bring the answers out

        2) <u>Zeno's method—Reductio ad Absurdum</u> (475BC)

            a) reducing alternative positions to their absurd conclusions

            b) can expose falsehood, doesn't always prove something true

        3) <u>Aristotle's method—Deduction</u> (384-322BC)

            a) argues from the general to the particular

                1) all men are mortal

                2) Socrates is a man

                3) therefore, Socrates is mortal

            b) the series of propositions is called a deductive syllogism

            c) strength = a valid deductive syllogism brings a certain conclusion

            d) weakness = universal or general propositions are rarely agreed upon

            e) we must settle for highly probable conclusions

    B) <u>The Modern World</u>

        1) <u>the inductive method</u> (argues from the particular to the universal)

            a) Francis Bacon (1561-1626) stressed it as a scientific tool

            b) he utilized it with scientific experimentation

            c) conclusions aren't certain unless all particulars are included

            d) the more particulars, the more probable the conclusion

        2) <u>the scientific method</u> (doesn't give absolute certainty)

            a) observation

            b) proposal of a question or problem

            c) hypothesis (educated guess)

            d) experimentation

            e) theory (a highly probable hypothesis)

            f) natural law (theory thought to be valid on a universal scale)

C) <u>Some Contemporary Methods</u>
    1) <u>the existential method</u>
        a) Soren Kierkegaard (1813-1855) "the father of modern existentialism"
        b) subjective truth more important than objective truth
        c) truth is personal, not propositional
        d) truth is found in experience, not in rational realm (leads to fideism)
        e) a leap of faith into non-rational realm
        f) Jean Paul Sartre (values are created, not discovered)
    2) <u>the phenomenological method</u>
        a) founded by Edmund Husserl (1859-1938)
        b) attempts to avoid all presuppositions
        c) let facts speak for themselves
        d) naive to presuppose it alone has no presuppositions
    3) <u>the analytic methods</u>
        a) <u>verificational method</u> (A. J. Ayer, 1910-1989)
            —for a statement to be true, it must be purely definitional or verifiable by one or more of the 5 senses; metaphysics is meaningless; logical positivism (self-refuting)
        b) <u>falsification principle</u> (Antony Flew, 1923-)
            —a statement is meaningless unless it is subject to falsification (invisible gardener)
        c) <u>clarification method</u>
            —Ludwig Wittgenstein (1889-1951)
            —philosophical puzzles solved by clarification of language; language games (clarification is not enough—what about truth?)
D) <u>Conclusion</u>—more than one way to discover truth; no philosophical methodology can eliminate the possibility of divine revelation

4) <u>The Tools of Philosophy</u> (chapter 4)

 —logic deals with the rules for proper argumentation

  A) <u>the nature of an argument</u>

    1) premises (the evidence)

    2) conclusion (follows from the evidence)

    3) arguments can be formal or informal

    4) example of a formal argument

      a) all men are mortal (premise #1)

      b) Socrates is a man (premise #2)

      c) therefore, Socrates is mortal (conclusion)

  B) <u>kinds of argument</u>

    1) <u>inductive</u> (argues from the part to the general)

      a) a good one will have a highly probable conclusion

      b) conclusion is thought of as probably true

      c) Socrates is a man; Socrates is mortal; therefore, all men are mortal (weak inductive argument)

    2) <u>deductive</u> (argues from the general to the particular)

      a) if valid, the premises guarantee the conclusion

      b) all men are mortal; Socrates is a man; Socrates is mortal (a valid deductive argument)

      c) <u>validity</u> (when argument is properly structured)

        1) arguments are valid or invalid

        2) statements are true or false

        3) arguments aren't true or false; their conclusions are true or false

        4) a valid argument might bring false conclusions

        5) a valid deductive argument with true premises will always bring a true conclusion

      d) <u>soundness</u> (a valid argument with true premises)

      e) <u>conclusive arguments</u> (premises known to be true)

      f) <u>reliable arguments</u> (a valid argument which has good evidence for the truth of its premises)

  C) <u>Clarity</u> (we must understand the meaning of a premise before determining if it is true)

    1) <u>definitions</u>

      a) <u>nominal</u>—when a word receives an arbitrary meaning; found in dictionary

      b) <u>real</u>—describe characteristics possessed by all members of a certain class, but not by anything outside that class

2) <u>analysis of concepts</u>
  a) goes beyond the definition of words
  b) seeks to observe the usage of these words in
   ordinary language

D) <u>Analytical & Synthetic Statements</u>
 1) <u>analytical statements</u>
  a) true by definition (tautologies)
  b) their denial is a contradiction
  c) they say nothing about the physical world
  d) "<u>a priori</u>" (self-evident prior to experience)
  e) all bachelors are unmarried males/1+1=2
 2) <u>synthetic statements</u>
  a) "<u>a posteriori</u>" (their truth is determined by an
   appeal to factual evidence)
  b) the evidence must be examined

E) <u>The Scientific Method</u> (deals with synthetic statements)
 1) formulate the statement clearly & carefully
 2) predict the implications of such a belief
 3) controlled experiments to test predictions
 4) accept or reject statement

F) <u>Deductive Syllogisms</u> (6 rules—pages 64-68)
 1) use only 3 terms; no term used in more than one sense
 2) middle term must refer to all members of it's class at
  least once in the premises
 3) no term can refer to all members of it's class in the
  conclusion, if it didn't in the premises
 4) cannot have 2 negative premises
 5) if one premise is negative, the conclusion must also be
  negative
 6) a particular conclusion cannot have 2 universal
  premises

5) <u>The Challenge of Philosophy</u> (chapter 5)

    A) <u>the challenge of philosophy in general</u>

        1) <u>philosophical examination</u>

            a) Socrates—"the unexamined life is not worth living"

            b) the philosopher seeks answers to basic questions about life (<u>life's purposes</u>—where did I come from?/why am I here? /where am I going?) (<u>life's presuppositions</u>—not what we think about, but what we think with)

        2) <u>clarification of thought</u>

            a) eliminating fallacious thinking

            b) defining ambiguous statements

        3) <u>argumentation</u>

            a) philosophy = the pursuit of truth

            b) argumentation = the strategy that directs that pursuit

            c) philosophy is dedicated to clear & correct argumentation

        4) <u>putting knowledge into a system</u>

            a) <u>a weltanschauung</u> (a world view)

                1) internal consistency (no contradictions)

                2) external comprehensiveness (accounts for all facts of experience)

                3) correspondence (fit all the facts together)

            b) <u>several world views</u> (theism, atheism, pantheism, polytheism, etc.)

    B) <u>the challenge of philosophy for a Christian</u>

        1) <u>twofold function for philosophy</u>

            a) constructing a Christian system of thought

            b) refuting contrary views

        2) <u>the biblical basis for Christian philosophy</u>

            a) 2 Cor 10:5; Col 2:8; 1 Cor 1:20; Mt 22:37; 1 Pt 3:15; Col 4:5-6; Ac 17:2; Ju 3; Titus 1:7-9; Rm 1:18-22; 2:14-15; Ps 19:1

            b) we must recognize error before we can refute it

            c) the Bible condemns the false philosophy of man

            d) not the true philosophy of God

3) <u>the roles of philosophy for a Christian</u>
    a) in theology (forming a Christian world view)
    b) in apologetics (defend against external threats)
    c) in polemics (defend against internal heresies)
    d) in communication
        1) learn to share gospel with people of different world views
        2) remove intellectual stumbling blocks
        3) present gospel in a clear, consistent manner

Part Two—Epistemology (what is knowledge?)

6) <u>Can We Know?</u> (Chapter 6)
    A) <u>Skepticism</u> (suspending judgment)
        1) epistemology—the issue is not what we believe, but what are we justified in believing
        2) a consistent skeptic never agrees with any premise & makes it impossible for an argument to get started
    B) <u>Different Types of Skepticism</u>
        1) <u>thoroughgoing or complete skepticism</u>
            a) we have no knowledge whatsoever
            b) <u>Sextus Empiricus</u> (150-225AD?)
                1) skepticism predates his thought
                2) his skepticism had three stages:
                    -<u>antithesis</u> (2 contradictory claims about same subject)
                    -<u>suspension of judgment</u>
                    -<u>ataraxia</u> (happiness, contentment, peace of mind, state of unperturbedness, freedom from dogmaticism)
            c) <u>David Hume</u> (1711-1776) an empiricist
                1) no generalization about experience is ever rationally justified (sunrise)
                2) his view attacks knowing with certainty
                3) we can still argue that the sun will probably rise tomorrow
        2) <u>mitigated skepticism</u>
            a) admits some limited kinds of knowledge
            b) Bishop John Wilkins (1614-1672) & Joseph Glanvill (1636-1680) members of a British science organization
            c) <u>infallibly certain knowledge</u>
                1) unattainable by man
                2) man's abilities may be defective/corrupted
            d) <u>indubitably certain knowledge</u> (this is possible)
                1) we can know beyond reasonable doubt
                2) Anglo-American theory of legal evidence
            e) <u>Immanuel Kant</u> (1724-1804)
                1) all knowledge begins with sense experience
                2) 3 sciences which are not possible:
                    a) science of a supposed real world
                    b) science of a supposed real self
                    c) science of God based upon pure reason

           3) cosmological argument fails

              —principle of causality may not apply to
                God (categories of mind/real world)

              —God is not an object of sense experience

           4) Kant embraced a metaphysical skepticism

           5) knower doesn't conform to object known

           6) object known conforms to knower

      3) <u>limited skepticism</u>

        —particular type of knowledge questioned

          a) <u>A. J. Ayer</u> (1910-1989)

             1) logical positivism/verification principle

             2) only 2 ways to know something:

                —true by definition; verified by senses

             3) therefore, metaphysics is meaningless

             4) verification principle fails its own tests

          b) <u>Antony Flew</u> (a leading British philosopher)

             1) falsification principle/invisible gardener

             2) any non-falsifiable belief is nonsense

             3) theology (study of God) is nonsense

             4) refutation—resurrection, miracles,
                predictions were falsifiable

      4) <u>methodological or Cartesian skepticism</u>

        —<u>Rene Descartes</u> (1596-1650)

          a) skepticism—the method whereby all doubt could
            be overcome

          b) he doubted everything until he found that which
            could not be doubted (absolute certainty)

          c) from there, he hoped to derive all knowledge

          d) the more he doubted, the more he recognized
            the existence of the doubter (cogito, ergo sum)

      5) <u>irrationalism</u> (some types of existentialism)

        —<u>Albert Camus</u> (1913-1960)

          a) he accepted Kierkegaard's skepticism concerning
            any rational attempts to explain the world

          b) he rejected Kierkegaard's leap of faith to find
            meaning (he agreed with Nietzsche's nihilism)

          c) no meaning, no objective knowledge or values

          d) the world is absurd

   B) <u>Arguments Against Skepticism</u>

      1) <u>skepticism is inconsistent (Augustine)</u>

          a) rationally inconsistent (the claim that man
            cannot know is itself a claim to know something)

  b) practically inconsistent (the skeptic can't live
   consistently with his skepticism)
2) <u>verificational principle fails its own test</u>
 —not purely definitional; not verifiable by 5 senses
3) <u>skepticism is against common sense</u>
 a) <u>Thomas Reid</u> (1710-1796)
  1) disagreed with David Hume's skepticism
  2) rational proofs for all beliefs—inappropriate
  3) need for justification must end somewhere
  4) basic beliefs are self-evident
 b) <u>John Pollock</u>-skepticism never agrees with
  common sense (rainfall, weather report)
4) <u>skepticism is in conflict with language</u>-when a skeptic
 expresses his doubt, he is not skeptical about the
 words he uses to do so
5) <u>skepticism is not a consequence of induction</u>
 a) deduction tries to guarantee a certain conclusion
 b) induction only seeks a probable conclusion
 c) why should we reject a probable conclusion when
  the evidence favors it?
C) <u>The Value of Skepticism</u>
 1) argues against any dogmaticism lacking good evidence
 2) skepticism raises 2 questions:
  —is there adequate evidence for my claim to know?
  —does my belief system have contradictions?
 3) if we claim to know something, the skeptic must be
  answered

7) <u>How Can We Know?</u> (Chapter 7)
   A) skeptical claims are unjustified
   B) <u>5 sources of our beliefs</u>
      1) <u>Faith or Authoritarianism</u>
         a) most common source of our beliefs
         b) the testimony of others
         c) we accept beliefs as justified when they seem to come from reliable sources
         d) our historical knowledge is based on others' testimonies
         e) the same is true of our knowledge of current events in foreign lands
         f) it is impossible for us to reason to & experience everything
         g) <u>evaluation of faith as only way to know</u>
            1) always possible to question an authority
            2) authorities often disagree
               a) 3 ways to measure authorities
                  1) prestige or credentials
                  2) number of authorities who agree
                  3) the persistence of the belief
               b) none of these 3 are totally conclusive
      2) <u>Subjectivism</u>
         a) the knower has some kind of direct contact with what is known
         b) if you experience it-you know it
         c) called <u>direct or common-sense realism</u>
         d) more sophisticated form-<u>phenomenology</u>-Husserl
         e) <u>mysticism</u>—seeing the unity of all things
         f) <u>evaluation of subjectivism as only way to know</u>
            1) usually leads to solipsism—the world exists only in my mind
            2) subjectivism can't declare any belief false
            3) experience alone is insufficient; our experiences must be interpreted
      3) <u>Rationalism</u>
         a) justification of our beliefs found in reason alone
         b) starting point must be rationally certain
         c) rationalists try to deduce the whole of reality
         d) <u>evaluation of reason as only way to know</u>
            1) reason—a good negative test for truth
               a) beliefs contrary to reason are false

    b) non-contradictory beliefs are not
     always true
    c) reason demonstrates what is possible,
     not actual
   2) no generally agreed starting point
    (Descartes, Spinoza, Leibniz)
   3) rationalists introduce hidden assumptions
    besides reason
   4) you cannot reason to first principles

4) Empiricism
  a) sense experience is the source of our knowledge
  b) weaker form—our senses give us some type of
   knowledge
  c) stronger form—all knowledge comes through
   sense experience
  d) our ideas & concepts are wholly derived from
   sense experiences
  e) John Locke—there is nothing in the intellect
   which was not first in the senses (Aquinas—
   except the intellect itself)
  f) David Hume—also reduced all ideas to empirical
   experiences
  g) Immanuel Kant—not an empiricist, but denied
   there is any knowledge of reality derived
   from pure reason alone
  h) evaluation of empriricism as only way to know
   1) it fails to account for all knowledge
   2) it often leads to skepticism (David Hume)
   3) universals can't be derived from
    experience alone
   4) ideas such as "equal" or "parallel" are never
    found in experience
   5) the knower must come equipped with
    concepts, or else he will not be able to
    interpret experiences

5) Pragmaticism
  a) ideas or beliefs that work are true
  b) ideas or beliefs that fail are false
  c) Wm James (1842-1910), Jn Dewey (1859-1952)
  d) evaluation of pragmaticism as only way to know
   1) lies often work, but are not true
   2) "X is useful" doesn't equal "X is true"

3) pragmaticism gives up objective grounds
for testing beliefs

C) <u>Conclusion</u>

1) none of the 5 methods can alone justify our beliefs

2) each method is best suited for a specific kind of
knowledge

a) <u>faith</u>—knowledge of past (testimony of others)

b) <u>intuition</u>—our sense of beauty/taste/ethics

c) <u>reason</u>—contradictions are false; source of our
beliefs concerning math, logic, universals

d) <u>experience</u>—knowledge of the external world

e) <u>pragmaticism</u>—regulates our behavior where
moral laws don't apply

8) <u>Is Certainty Possible?</u> (Chapter 8)
   A) <u>kinds of certainty</u>
      1) <u>apodictic certainty</u> (highest standard for certainty)
         a) logically necessary truth (absolutely certain)
         b) indubitability—exclusion of any doubt
         c) incorrigibility—incapable of being corrected
      2) <u>psychological certainty</u> (when knower feels certain)
      3) <u>conventional certainty</u> (attained by consulting a
         dictionary or an authority on the subject; bachelor =
         unmarried male, field goal = 3 points)
      4) <u>pragmatic certainty</u> (we feel certain of our beliefs if
         they work)
      5) <u>probability</u> (some believe certainty is impossible; they
         settle for probability)
   B) <u>types of knowledge & their relation to certainty</u>
      1) <u>moral commands</u>
         a) <u>moral relativism</u> (denial of moral absolutes)
         b) <u>response of moral absolutists</u>
            1) greater agreement between cultures than
              relativists admit (discourage cowardice)
           2) disagreements about morality doesn't
              mean there is no absolute moral law
           3) if moral relativism is true, then we can't
              condemn Hitler's actions
      2) <u>knowledge about the external world</u>
         a) <u>arguments for certainty</u>
            1) <u>Descartes</u>-a rationalist; external world must
              exist as cause of my idea of external world
           2) <u>G. E. Moore</u>-an empiricist; my body is proof
              an external world of physical objects exists
         b) <u>arguments against certainty</u>
            1) most philosophers believe in the existence
              of the external world
           2) still, they would not consider this
              knowledge to be certain
           3) <u>Hume</u>-it is rationally possible that nothing
              exists; existence of external world is only
              probable
      3) <u>self-awareness</u> (knowledge of the self by the self)
         a) <u>arguments for the certainty of self-awareness</u>
            1) <u>Descartes</u>-the more I doubt, the more I am
              aware of the existence of the doubter

2) <u>John Locke</u>-everytime we think, we become conscious of our own existence

b) <u>arguments against certainty of self-awareness</u>

    1) <u>Gilbert Ryle</u>-we can never fully describe ourselves; we don't know & can't remember everything about ourselves

4) <u>logical & mathematical knowledge</u>

    a) <u>arguments for the certainty of logic & math</u>

        1) many philosophers believe this knowledge is true in every possible world

        2) the denial of these truths involves a contradiction

    b) <u>arguments against certain knowledge in these areas</u>

        1) some believe these truths depend on form alone

        2) logic tells us what is possible & impossible

        3) logic cannot tell us what is actual

        4) logic & math tell us nothing about the real world

        5) <u>John Stuart Mill</u>-just because we can't conceive of another set of logical laws doesn't make this other set impossible

        6) <u>W. V. O. Quine</u>- even those beliefs we hold with the greatest certainty could turn out to be false

C) <u>Conclusion</u>

  1) human knowledge is fallible & probable in most respects

  2) only God can know everything with total certainty

  3) humans may have some certain knowledge

  4) good philosophers disagree concerning its nature & extent

  5) God's Word is infallible, but man's knowledge of it isn't

  6) man cannot have certain knowledge of God

  7) the difference between certainty & certitude

    a) <u>certainty</u>-impossible in matters of experience (only probable knowledge is possible)

    b) <u>certitude</u>-added assurance given to believers by internal testimony of Holy Spirit (Rm 8:16)

9) <u>How Do We Perceive the External World</u>? (Chapter 9)

   A) <u>Realism</u>

      1) <u>Extreme or Primitive Realism</u>

         a) the view of the common man

         b) every experienced object exists independently of any observer (if I perceive it, its real)

         c) <u>evaluation</u>—everyone has been wrong in a judgment about a perception

         d) can't account for illusions or hallucinations

      2) <u>Common-Sense Realism</u>

         a) agrees with primitive realism that physical objects are independent of or external to the mind

         b) agrees with primitive realism that physical objects are directly & immediately observable to the mind

         c) disagrees by viewing the unreal, illusory, or hallucinations as subjective objects occuring exclusively in the mind

         d) <u>problems</u>—how do we know all perceptions aren't illusions?

         e) <u>problems</u>—how can we be mistaken about real objects that are directly observable to the mind?

   B) <u>Dualism</u>

      1) <u>Representative Perception/Copy Theory of Knowledge</u>

         a) Descartes, Locke, Hume

         b) 2 distinct & independent orders of existence

            1) ideas (sense data)

            2) an independent & external world

         c) this view explains illusions
—pond on hot highway/stick in water

         d) this view explains perceptual relativity
—a round coin can look eliptical

         e) <u>problems with this view</u>

            1) no perception can be proven or disproven

            2) it leads to skepticism about real world

            3) distinction between real object & perceived object

            4) distinction between real space & time, & perceived space & time

2) <u>Phenomenalism</u> (A. J. Ayer)
      a) sense data language (we state how things appear to us; not how things really are)
      b) <u>problems with this view</u> (leads to agnosticism)
          1) why remove ourselves in such a way from reality? (questions of reality are left open)
          2) we can only say how reality appears to us

C) <u>Idealism</u>
  1) the view that material objects don't exist independently of some consciousness of them
  2) all reality is reduced exclusively to conscious beings and their states
  3) <u>the weaker form</u> Bishop George Berkeley (1685-1753)
      a) there is no independent world or reality outside of experience
      b) to be is to be perceived (reduces world to subjectivity)
      c) so called physical states-shared by several minds
      d) subjective experiences-only one perceiver sees it
      e) still, both physical & subjective states have no existence outside conscious experience
      f) does an object not perceived go out of existence?
      g) no, God always perceives all objects everywhere
      h) <u>problems</u>—makes God a deceiver since no material world exists & no one can live consistently as an idealist
  4) <u>the stronger form</u>
      a) more than the world is reduced to subjectivity
      b) even the self is reduced to subjectivity
      e) <u>problem</u>—no one can live consistently with this

D) <u>Conclusion</u>
  1) skepticism results if we cannot guarantee the relationship between the realm of ides & a material world
  2) though realism has problems, some sophisticated form of it best fits with common sense
  3) physiology, the psychology of perception, the natural sciences & their study of the functioning of the world can help to explain errors in perception

10) <u>How Are Beliefs Justified</u>? (Chapter 10)
    A) <u>Foundationalism</u>
        1) foundational beliefs are in need of no support
        2) they are sometimes called "self-evident truths"
        3) foundational beliefs support the rest of knowledge
        4) epistemic justification is like a pyramid
        5) beliefs on lowest tier are justifiably believed without
            appeal to any other reason
        6) beliefs in the higher tiers are ultimately justified by
            these lowest tier foundational beliefs
        7) <u>support for foundationalism</u>
            a) only 2 alternatives to foundationalism:
                1) circular justification
                2) an infinite regress of justification
            b) both alternatives are absurd
            c) justification must come to an end, or no belief is
                justified
            d) there may be some self-evident truths
            e) some premises are self-justified since they
                cannot be denied without contradiction
        8) <u>criticisms of foundationalism</u>
            a) no incorrigible statements that can be
                foundational (response-justification must stop
                somewhere; not all knowledge is capable of
                incorrigible foundations)
            b) there are no directly justified beliefs
            c) foundational beliefs aren't logically necessary
                —response-we should not require all
                    justification to be logically necessary
            d) foundationalism leads to dogmaticism (response-
                everyone is dogmatic)
            e) too few foundational beliefs to form a
                comprehensive epistemology
            f) theory-ladenness (the view that all our beliefs
                are effected by theory; even facts are
                theory-laden; if true, no foundations)
                1) response-the closer one's theory is to
                    reality, the less theory-laden it is
                2) the least theory-laden beliefs are
                    foundational

B) <u>Coherentism or Contextualism</u>
    1) knowledge viewed as a web of beliefs (not a pyramid)
    2) a mutual relationship between various beliefs
    3) A supports B; B supports C; C supports A
    4) beliefs closer to the center of the web are given up
       more reluctantly
    5) <u>support for coherentism</u>
       a) any objection against foundationalism
       b) the claim that there are no immediately justified
         beliefs
    6) <u>criticisms of coherentism</u>
       a) it leads to an infinite regress in justification
       b) ultimately, all beliefs fail to be justified
       c) coherentism is cut off from the real world since a
         person can be justified believing anything
C) <u>Conclusion</u>
    1) there are Christian empistemologists on both sides
    2) agreement can be found
       a) if foundationalists will allow basic beliefs that
         are not incorrigible & logically necessary
       b) if coherentists will acknowledge that beliefs at
         the outer edges of the web are farther from
         experience
    3) a Christian cannot accept agnosticism or relativism
       about the real world

Part Three—Metaphysics (What is Reality?)

11) <u>Is Reality One or Many</u>? (Chapter 11)
    A) if reality is one, how do we explain multiplicity?
    B) if reality is many, how do we explain unity?
    C) <u>Monism (reality is one but not many)</u>
        1) <u>Parmenides</u> (ancient Greek philosopher)
            a) things cannot differ by non-being (nothing)
            b) things cannot differ by being (all things exist)
        2) <u>Zeno</u> (famous pupil of Parmenides)
            a) if reality is many, absurdities follow
            b) movement is impossible
                1) space—both finite & infinite (points A & B)
                2) race between tortoise & Achilles (give the
                    tortoise the lead & Achilles will never
                    catch up)
        3) <u>replies to monism</u>
            a) Zeno—may be a point at which space can no
                longer be split
            b) Parmenides—things can differ in being & still be
                genuinely different (Aquinas—act/potency)
    D) <u>Pluralism (reality is many)</u>
        1) <u>Atomism</u> (things differ by absolute non-being)
            a) Democritus & Leucippus
            b) reality is made up of innumerable & indivisible
                atoms which fill the void of space
            c) the void is pure emptiness (absolutely nothing)
            d) each atom differs from another by occupying
                different places in empty space
            e) <u>criticism</u>—to differ by absolute non-being is to
                differ by absolutely nothing
            f) <u>criticism</u>—space is not an empty container
            g) unless there is a real difference in being,
                Parmenides & monism win
        2) <u>Platonism</u> (things differ by relative non-being)
            a) the ultimate things in the universe are ideal
                forms or ideas
            b) all differentiation is by negation (otherness)
            c) the pencil is not everything else
            d) <u>criticism</u>—differing by non-being is differing by
                nothing; if all differentiation is by negation,
                then everything in the universe must be
                negated to identify something

3) <u>Aristotle</u> (things differ in their being, which is simple)
    a) the ultimate items of the universe are not atoms
    b) the ultimate items are Unmoved Movers (gods)
    c) Unmoved Movers are simple beings (pure forms of being)
    d) simple = uncomposed of form & matter
    e) Unmoved Movers literally differ in being
    f) <u>criticism</u>—recognized by Aristotle—a universe with multiple gods would have no unity
    g) <u>criticism</u>—simple beings are pure beings & do not differ as such

4) <u>Aquinas</u> (things differ in their being, which is composed)
    a) argued for both unity & diversity within finite being itself
    b) finite being is complex & compound; it is composed of actuality & potentiality
    c) different potentials are <u>real</u> (they make a real difference in the kind of being a thing is)
    d) man-potential for being rational (tomatoes don't)
    e) Parmenides begs the question (he assumes that being always means entirely the same thing in an attempt to prove monism)
    f) Aquinas understood being as analogous (similar)
    g) there are many different beings that share in being
    h) there can be many different beings since they have differing potentials
    i) unity in being—only one thing is Being (God)
    j) everything else has differing potentials
    k) God is pure actuality; everything else has act/potency

E) <u>Plotinus (unity goes beyond being)</u>
    1) Plotinus was a pantheist (all reality is the One/god)
    2) God is the One that goes beyond all being, knowledge, & consciousness
    3) all multiplicity & all being flows from the One
    4) different degrees of being, depends on degree of unity
        a) Mind/Nous-most unified of all beings
        b) World Soul-comes next
        c) matter-last in the chain of being
    5) <u>criticism</u>—if being is that which is real, if the One is real, then it is not really beyond being

F) <u>The Christian Trinity as a Model for the One & the Many</u>
    1) unity = one God; plurality = 3 Persons
    2) God is a unity & diversity
    3) <u>criticism</u>—the fact that God is 3 Persons doesn't explain
        how there can be many beings in the universe

G) <u>Conclusion</u>
    1) <u>monism</u>—only one being in the universe
    2) <u>pluralism</u>—many beings in the universe
    3) <u>Christian theists</u>
        a) a real unity & diversity of being in the universe
        b) unity of being—God is the one Being from whom
            all other beings derive their existence
        c) diversity of being—beings are similar (analogous),
            but not identical to one another

12) <u>The Relationship Between Mind & Body</u> (Chapter 12)
   A) <u>the significance of this topic</u>
      1) if men are robots, then morality & law are misguided
      2) if man is merely material, then religion is false
   B) <u>Monistic Theories of Man</u>
      1) <u>extreme materialism</u> (we are our bodies)
         a) man is identical to his body
         b) we cease to exist at physical death
         c) criticisms
            1) guilt is moral, but not physical (which part of our body is guilty?)
            2) mental predicates—which part of our body loves or is angry?
            3) the whole man appears to be more than his body (guilty, loving, angry)
            4) epistemological predicates-truth/falsehood can't be determined soley on a physical basis
            5) what does a thought look like? (love?)
      2) <u>the identity theory</u>
         a) mentalistic terms & physicalistic terms have different connotative meanings, but they ultimately refer to physical phenomena
         b) science will eventually prove that mental states are identical with brain states
         c) criticisms
            1) it is absurd to ask for the location of a mental event
            2) if mental events are physical, then why does subject alone have access to them?
      3) <u>idealism</u> (the opposite of extreme materialism)
         a) Bishop George Berkeley
         b) the mind & its perceptions are the only things that exist (man is reducible to mind, not matter)
         c) criticism—incoherent/impractical view of reality
      4) <u>the double-aspect theory</u>
         a) the physical & the mental are actually different aspects of something that is neither physical nor mental (some philosophers would say it is both) Benedict Spinoza (1632-1677)
         b) criticisms—underlying unity left unexplained & no definition for the word "aspect"

C) <u>Dualistic Theories of Man</u>
    1) <u>Interactionism</u> (most common & simple dualistic view)
        a) human being is mind & body in this present state
        b) mental events may cause physical events
            (sorrow, tears)
        c) bodily events may cause mental events
            (song, joy)
        d) Rene Descartes—2 kinds of substance in man
        e) criticisms
            1) contradicts energy conservation (response-
                no loss or gain of physical energy occurs
                with mental acts)
            2) physical can't effect mental & visa versa
                (response-why assume that a cause must
                contain same properties as its effect?; elec-
                trical activity can cause a magnetic field)
            3) some say only the physical can cause the
                mental (epiphenomenalism)
    2) <u>Parallelism</u> (no direct or indirect interaction between
    mind & body)
        a) every mental event is systematically correlated
            with some physical event, but neither is the
            cause of the other
        b) criticisms
            1) could such a high degree of correlation be
                purely accidental?
            2) one-to-one correspondence fails (coma-
                mental activity ceases but bodily activity
                does not)
    3) <u>Preestablished Harmony</u> (Leibniz—no causal relations)
      —a variation of parallelism (same problems)
    4) <u>Occasionalism</u> (Augustine)
        a) when we mentally will to move our arm, then on
            that occasion God physically moves our arm
        b) no causal relationship between mental/physical
        c) it is the result of God's activity
        d) God causes all events
        e) criticisms
            1) is God deceiving us? (is mind-body
                relationship an illusion?)
            2) Bible—God can supernaturally intervene,
                but He usually uses secondary means to
                accomplish His purposes (procreation)

5) <u>Epiphenomenalism</u>
    a) only physical events can cause mental events
       (not visa versa)
    b) unlike materialism, there are genuine mental
       events
    c) still, mental events depend on physical causes
    d) future science will prove this view correct
    e) criticisms—mental events do appear to cause
       physical events & they admit their evidence
       is yet to be found

D) <u>Conclusion</u>
    1) biblical view—man is not reducible to matter
    2) Christian dichotomy (body & soul)
    3) Christian trichotomy (body, soul, spirit)

13) <u>Is Man Free</u>? (Chapter 13)
  —<u>Incompatibilist Freedom</u> (no prior conditions determine a
        free action; freedom & determinism cannot be reconciled)
  —<u>Compatibilist Freedom</u> (an action can still be free even if
        prior conditions determined what it would be)
  A) <u>Determinism</u> (all events are governed by laws)
      1) <u>Hard Determinism</u>-all human activity is ruled by
          heredity & enviroment (an incompatibilist position)
          a) not fatalism (the inevitable will happen
                regardless of what we do or do not do)
          b) hard determinism—our actions do effect what
                happens, but even our actions are determined
                by prior causes
          c) criticisms—denies human free will (no freedom to
                do otherwise) & moral responsibility (can we
                really punish criminals?)
      2) <u>Soft Determinism</u>-a compatibilist position (freedom &
          determinism can be reconciled)
          a) prior conditions may determine our action, yet
                our action is still free
          b) we are free & responsible for any actions that
                are without external constraint
          c) criticisms—our desires, character, & will are still
                determined; not really free to do otherwise
  B) <u>Simple Indeterminism</u>-few supporters, least likely view
      1) an incompatibilist position that denies determinism
      2) our free actions are uncaused events (no prior causes)
      3) criticisms—leaves no reason or cause for our actions;
          retains freedom, but not responsibility
  C) <u>Libertarianism</u> (man is genuinely free to do otherwise)
      1) an incompatibilist position that denies determinism
      2) our free actions are not caused by another
      3) our free actions are not uncaused (denies simple
          indeterminism)
      4) our free actions are self-caused (self-determination)
      5) criticisms—many deny the idea of an immaterial self;
          many believe man is not a substance, but a
          collection of events (Hume, Gordon Clark)
  D) <u>The Two-Level Theory</u>
      1) determinism & free will are in some sense
          independent of each other
      2) events are determined (they have causes)

     3) human actions are not determined (they are not
         caused, but they do have reasons or purposes)
     4) criticisms-many deny the idea of immaterial self;
         reasons & causes are very closely related

E) Christian Views of Determinism & Free Will
     1) hyper-Calvinism (Gordon Clark)
         a) God predetermines every event
         b) man is not free to do otherwise
     2) Calvinism (most Calvinists)
         —man is free to choose according to his nature
           (fallen or regenerate)
     3) extreme Arminianism (Clark Pinnock)
         —God does not foreknow future free choices
     4) classical Arminianism (most Arminians)
         —God foreknows what we will freely choose to do
     5) the Divine Mystery View (Geisler)
         a) God predetermines every event
         b) still, man is free to do otherwise
         c) reconciliation of Divine predestination & human
           free will goes beyond human reason
     6) Molinism (Middle Knowledge) (Craig)
         a) God knows what we would freely choose in every
           possible world
         b) God's predestining act—actualizing the possible
           world that best fulfills His purposes
         c) God predetermines the course of history
         d) still, man freely chooses his actions

14) <u>Does Man Survive Death</u>/ (Chapter 14)

    A) <u>Arguments Against Immortality</u>

        1) <u>the universality of human mortality</u>

            a) no one doubts that all humans die

            b) the real question = what follows death?

        2) <u>the analogy of nature</u> (Hume)

            a) bodily changes produce proportionate changes in our minds; total death of the body will entail the total death of the mind

            b) nothing in nature can survive a drastic change in enviroment; can the mind survive without the body?

            c) animals resemble humans (animals aren't immortal)

            d) the world is destructible; so is man's mind

            e) criticisms—assumes the conclusion; everyone agrees in the mortality of physical realm; many differences between animals & man

        3) <u>the body-mind dependence argument</u> (B. Russell)

            a) most impressive argument against immortality

            b) activity of mind is now dependent on the body

            c) our mental life is dependent on brain activity

            d) our brains will eventually die

            e) criticism—the present body-mind dependence says nothing about the conditions of future existence

    B) <u>Types of Immortality Doctrines</u>

        1)<u>Plato's immortal soul doctrine</u>

            a) the human soul is immortal

            b) the soul is the real person

            c) no future resurrection

        2) <u>the shadow-man or minimal person doctrine</u>

            a) the real person is the soul

            b) it can survive without the body

            c) accepts a future resurrection

        3) <u>the reconstruction doctrine</u>

            a) we do not exist without our bodies

            b) our bodies will be resurrected after death

            c) God will call us back into existence

            d) soul sleep doctrine (Jehovah's Witnesses)

C) Defense of the Shadow-Man Doctrine
    1) Socrates
        a) only composite things like bodies decompose
        b) the soul is simple & does not come apart
    2) Plato
        a) eternal ideas (the forms are eternal/unchanging)
            1) they are the real objects of knowledge
            2) the soul knows the forms
            3) the soul is probably eternal & unchanging
        b) reminiscence (we know certain things a priori)
            1) Plato argued the soul preexisted the body
            2) Christians must reject this view
    3) C. S. Lewis
        a) rationality could not have been caused by purely
            material causes
        b) hence, rationality is supernatural & immaterial
    4) near death experiences (Habermas & Moreland)
    5) recent brain research (decisions not made in the brain)
    6) Jesus' resurrection (guarantees immortality)
D) Objections to Arguments for Immortality
    1) even if the soul cannot change, maybe it can still cease
        to exist?
    2) why must the knower resemble the thing known?
    3) the problem of identity (memory; is the soul the same
        person after death?)
    4) our present way of individuating persons is by way of
        their bodies (this says nothing about the hereafter)
    5) some reduce mental states to the physical
    6) sense experience is impossible without a body (maybe
        a more direct way of knowing will be possible
        without the hindrance of our bodies?)
    7) where is the afterlife? (no logical reason to deny the
        afterlife is in non-physical realm, though it could be
        in the physical realm)
E) Conclusion
    1) no decisive evidence against immortality
    2) for Christians, Christ's resurrection settles the issue
    3) the minimal person survives the death of the body
        (Lk 16; 2 Cor 5:8)
    4) at the resurrection, the minimal person is reunited
        with its resurrection body

15) <u>Are There Other Minds?</u> (Chapter 15)
    A) <u>arguments for other minds based on analogy</u>
        1) the mental states we experience are associated with
            our bodies & their behavior
        2) other bodies similar to ours display similar behavior
        3) we assume that there are mental states associated
            with other bodies similar to our own mental states
        4) <u>criticisms</u>
            a) arguments based on analogy are usually weak
            b) no way to verify this argument
            c) the argument is circular (not as circular as its
               denial)
        5) <u>defense of the argument from analogy</u> (A. J. Ayer)
            a) verbal communication confirms this argument
               (people explain their mental states in much
               the same way that we understand our own)
            b) the argument can be directly checked (others
               rightly conclude we are in pain when we
               scream)
            c) we don't need public phenomena to verify a
               private experience (mental thoughts)
        6) <u>alternate form of the argument from analogy</u>
            a) an effect often resembles its cause
            b) other beings display rational activity
            c) rational activity only comes from rational minds
    B) <u>other arguments for the existence of other minds</u>
        1) <u>Behaviorism</u> (B. F. Skinner) all mental states are fully
            reducible to physical states (the mind = the brain)
        2) <u>Ludwig Wittgenstein</u>—words are used as symbols for
            sense perceptions
    C) <u>conclusion</u>
        1) the argument from analogy has been criticized in
            contemporary thought
         2) still, it seems to be as defensible as any other
            argument for other minds
        3) <u>my argument</u>—the denial of other minds cannot be
            communicated without affirming the existence of
            other minds

16) <u>What is Truth?</u> (Chapter 16)

    A) <u>the coherence theory of truth</u>

        1) something is true only if it does not contradict statements in its own system of thought

        2) statements are either partially true or partially false

        3) the entire system of statements is wholly true

        4) <u>evaluation</u>

            a) non-contradiction is necessary if something is to be true

            b) still, a statement can be consistent with its system & still be false

            c) coherent statement might not apply to real world

            d) logically possible to have 2 coherent systems

            e) no such thing as partial truth or partial falsehood

    B) <u>the pragmatic theory of truth</u> (truth is whatver works)

        1) <u>Charles Sanders Pierce</u> (truth is the practical consequence of experimentation by the scientific community)

        2) <u>William James</u> (truth is determined by personal & practical consequences; truth is whatever works for the individual)

        3) <u>John Dewey</u> (truth is mutable; ideas become true when the facts are in)

        4) <u>evaluation</u>

            a) <u>Pierce</u>—his statement is itself neither true nor false by its own criterion

            b) <u>James</u>—lies often work, but aren't true; doctors often lie to help patients recover

            c) <u>Dewey</u>—denial of absolutes is absurd; a Monday crime didn't occur until proven on Friday

    C) <u>the performance theory of truth</u> (P. F. Strawson)

        1) we perform an action when we make truth claims

        2) "it is true that it is raining" = "I agree that it is raining"

        3) <u>criticism</u>—doesn't account for blind use of word "truth"

        4) agreeing that something is true does not make it true

    D) <u>the correspondence theory of truth</u> (when a statement corresponds to reality)

        1) <u>Aristotle</u>—a statement is true if it says of what is, that it is; or of what is not, that it is not. a statement is false if it says of what is, that it is not; or of what is not, that it is

2) <u>Alfred Tarski</u> (truth is a property of a sentence, when the sentence expresses the genuine state of a reality)

3) <u>G. E. Moore</u> (truth is the facts, but no such things as true propositions) this view is incoherent

E) <u>conclusion</u>—only the correspondence theory of truth is adequate; all other theories result in relativism or agnosticism

Part Four—Philosophy of Religion
(What is the Ultimate?)

17) <u>The Relationship Between Faith & Reason</u> (Chapter 17)
    A) <u>Revelation</u>—God supernaturally revealing truth (faith)
    B) <u>Reason</u>—the human mind's natural ability to discover truth
    C) <u>Revelation Only</u> (faith only) {fideism}
        1) <u>Soren Kierkegaard</u> (1813-1855)
            a) father of modern existentialism
            b) man is incapable of discovering divine truth
            c) God is wholly other
            d) Christian truth—found only through a leap of
                faith against all reason (an act of the will)
            e) attempts to prove God's existence are futile
            f) whether Jesus rose in history is unimportant
            g) subjective belief is all that matters
            h) subjective beliefs are more important than
                objective truth
        2) <u>Karl Barth</u> (1886-1968) {neo-orthodoxy}
            a) agreed with Kierkegaard that God is wholly other
            b) attempts to reason to God are futile, but God has
                supernaturally revealed Himself to man
            c) the Bible becomes the Word of God to us through
                an existential encounter (can't be verbalized)
            d) the Bible contains errors
            e) God has not revealed Himself to man in nature
            f) even if He did, fallen man would distort this
    D) <u>Reason Only</u>
        1) <u>Immanuel Kant</u> (1724-1804)
            a) by pure, speculative reason—no way to find God
            b) by practical, moral reason—we must live as if God
                exists (we must postulate God's existence to
                make sense of our moral duty in this life)
            c) reason demands we live as if miracles don't occur
        2) <u>Benedict Spinoza</u> (1632-1677)
            a) all truth known only through self-evident axioms
            b) truth only known through pure reason
            c) ontological argument—God must exist
            d) he was a pantheist (God is the universe)
            e) he was a monist—only one being exists
            f) evil is an illusion; miracles are impossible (they
                violate the unchangable laws of nature)

E) <u>Reason Over Revelation</u>
    1) <u>Alexandrian Fathers</u> (early church leaders)
        a) <u>Justin Martyr</u> (100-165)
            —he Christianized ancient Greek philosophers
        b) <u>Clement of Alexandria</u> (150-215)
            1) before Christ, philosophy saved the Greeks
            2) Plato spoke through the inspiration of God
            3) denial of literal millennium
    2) <u>modern higher criticism</u>
        a) liberals who critiqued the Bible & subjected it to
            human reason to find errors in it
        b) the Bible contained God's Word & human errors
        c) Julius Wellhausen (1844-1918)
            —documentary hypothesis—denied Mosaic
            authorship of the Pentateuch
    3) <u>deists</u> (reject miracles)
        a) God created universe, but doesn't intervene
        b) Thomas Jefferson—removed miracles from NT

F) <u>Revelation over Reason</u>
    1) <u>Tertullian</u> (155-220)
        a) "what indeed has Athens to do with Jerusalem?"
        b) philosophers were the fathers of all heresies
        c) Christian should reason about revelation, not
            against it
        d) held to reason within boundaries of revelation
    2) <u>Cornelius Van Til</u> (1895-1987)
        a) must presuppose Christianity for reason to
            function properly in communication, science, life
        b) God is not subject to the laws of logic

G) <u>Revelation and Reason</u>
    1) <u>Augustine</u> (354-430)
        a) a background of Platonic philosophy/rationalism
        b) faith is understanding's step (trust in God
            initiates our knowledge of divine truth)
        c) understanding is faith's reward (more complete
            knowledge of truth)
        d) still, one must have some understanding of what
            something is before one believes it
        e) one can still prove God's existence
            1) unchanging truths exist in my mind
            2) my mind is changing
            3) a changing mind cannot produce
               unchanging truths

     4) hence, an unchanging Mind is the cause of
      unchanging truths
   f) man's sinful nature blinds him to God's truth
   g) faith leads a man into a fuller understanding of
    God's revelation
  2) <u>Thomas Aquinas</u> (1224-1274)
    a) background in Aristotle's philosophy/empiricism
    b) Aquinas started with sense experience/physical
     world (Augustine started with realm of ideas)
    c) still, Aquinas considered himself a follower of
     Augustine, but Aquinas stressed reason more
    d) Aquinas—sin hasn't fully destroyed man's reason
    e) some Christian truths can be proven
    f) 5 ways to prove God's existence:
     1) from movement to an unmoved Mover
     2) from effects to an uncaused Cause
     3) from contingent beings to necessary Being
     4) from degrees of perfection in finite beings
      to an infinitely perfect Being
     5) from mindless nature moving towards
      defined goals to a Mind that guides nature
    g) some Christian truths can only be known by faith
     (doctrine of the Trinity)
    h) belief that God exists (through reason alone)
    i) belief in God (through revelation/faith alone)
H) <u>Conclusion</u>
 1) impossible to totally separate reason & revelation
  a) we cannot be prove everything
  b) something must be presupposed (accepted by faith)
 2) confusion between "belief in" and "belief that"
 3) distinction between epistemology & ontology
  a) <u>epistemology</u> (how we know reality)
   —reason to revelation
  b) <u>ontology</u> (reality) —revelation over reason
 4) <u>some truth to all 5 views</u> (reason & revelation is best)
  a) reason—epistemologically prior to revelation
  b) revelation over reason (once revelation is found)
  c) revelation only—true in the sense that all truth
   ultimately comes from God (natural &
   supernatural revelation)
  d) reason only—true in the sense that reason must
   determine whether the supposed revelation is
   from God

5) <u>revelation & reason is the best view</u>
    a) assigns each to its own proper role
    b) shows their proper interrelationship
    c) no faith should be unreasonable
    d) reason cannot a priori reject revelation

18) <u>What is Meant by God?</u> (Chapter 18) <u>Different Ways to View God</u>
   A) <u>Theism</u>—God is both beyond & in the world
      1) Judaism, Islam, & Christianity
      2) God is transcendent (beyond & separate from world)
      3) God is immanent (involved with world;
         miracles/sustains the world)
      4) God is a personal God (an intelligent & moral Being)
      5) God created the universe out of nothing
      6) God alone is a totally independent Being (Necessary)
      7) all other beings are contingent
      8) God can perform miracles
   B) <u>Deism</u>—God is beyond, but not in the world
      1) God is transcendent, but not immanent
      2) Thomas Jefferson was a deist (cut miracles out of NT)
      3) God created universe, but doesn't intervene
      4) God doesn't or cannot perform miracles
      5) problem—creation is greatest miracle
      6) problem—natural laws are descriptive, not prescriptive
   C) <u>Pantheism</u>—God is in the world, but not beyond it
     1) all types of pantheism are monistic
     2) reality is ultimately one being
     3) <u>different types of pantheism</u>
       a) <u>absolute pantheism</u>—Parmenides-all things are one; all
          diversity is an illusion (being & non-being)
       b) <u>emanational pantheism</u>—Plotinus-all multiplicity
          unfolds from the One; God is beyond all being
       c) <u>multilevel pantheism</u>—Hinduism-Brahman is the
          highest level of reality, beyond all multiplicity &
          materiality. Brahman is manifested on lower levels.
          The world is not total illusion, but it is the lowest
          degree of reality (Maya).
       d) <u>modal pantheism</u>—Spinoza-only one absolute substance
          in universe; everything else is only a mode or
          moment of it.
       e) <u>developmental pantheism</u>—Hegel-Absolute Spirit
          unfolds itself through the developments of history
     4) <u>common elements in Pantheism</u>
       a) God is non-personal (a force)
       b) creation is out of God (not out of nothing)
       c) only one being exists (monism)
       d) God is the universe
       e) evil is not real; it is an illusion

       5) <u>problems with pantheism</u>
          a) pantheists must trust their senses like everyone else;
              our senses tell us reality is many
          b) Parmenides thought Being was univocal; actually there
              is one infinite Being, but many finite beings
          c) no one can live like evil is an illusion
          d) if creation is out of God, then why is God unlimited
              while creation is limited?
          e) pantheists deny individual souls while affirming
              reincarnation (which requires individual souls)
          f) cannot consistently communicate the idea that only one
              mind exists
D) <u>Panentheism</u>—the universe is God's body (process theology)
       1) Alfred North Whitehead & Charles Hartshorne
       2) God has 2 poles (potential & actual)
          a) potential pole = eternal & infinite
          b) actual pole = finite & changing (God's body)
       3) panentheism is a type of finite godism
       4) God & the world are interdependent
       5) the world is progressively getting better
       6) creation is a continual process of forming pre-existing
          matter; God is not creator, but directs world process
       7) panentheists reject the God of Theism (not personal
          enough—He doesn't change)
       8) <u>problems with panentheism</u>
          a) God cannot be both finite & infinite in His basic
              nature (Jesus has 2 natures)
          b) destroys God's sovereignty (dependent on world)
          c) no potential can actualize itself (empty cup or
              formless clay)
          d) world doesn't seem to be getting better
          e) God cannot guarantee the defeat of evil
          f) why worship a finite, non-sovereign god?
E) <u>Finite Godism</u>—a limited god beyond the universe
     1) Plato's Demiurge & Aristotle's 47 or 55 unmoved movers
     2) god is limited in either power, goodness, or both (due to
       the existence of evil)
     3) Rabbi Kushner—we must aid God if evil is to be defeated
     4) <u>other types of finite godism</u>
       1) <u>dualism</u>—two limited gods
       2) <u>polytheism</u>—many limited gods
       3) <u>henotheism</u>—many limited gods, but one is supreme

     5) <u>problems with finite godism</u>
         1) finite god/gods—dependent & needs an infinite Cause
         2) finite god/gods cannot guarantee defeat of evil
         3) existence of evil does not prove God is finite
F) <u>Atheism</u>—God does not exist
         1) impossible for God to exist (contradictory attributes)
         2) evil is incompatible with God
         3) widespread nonbelief diproves God's existence
G) <u>Agnosticism</u>—man cannot (or does not) know if God exists
     —self-refuting
H) <u>Skepticism</u>—we should suspend judgment about God
         1) skeptics claim to reject dogmaticism
         2) but they are dogmatic about their skepticism

19) <u>Does God Exist?</u> (Chapter 19)

   A) <u>Arguments for God's Existence</u>

      1) <u>Augustine's argument from unchangeable truths</u>

         a) eternal, unchangeable truths exist (7 + 3 = 10)

         b) temporal, changeable minds cannot account for the existence of eternal, unchangeable truths

         c) only an eternal, unchangeable Mind can cause the existence of eternal, unchangeable truths

      2) <u>Descartes' argument from imperfection</u>

         a) I have imperfect ideas (doubts, mistakes)

         b) one cannot know an idea is imperfect unless he has a knowledge of the idea of perfection

         c) an imperfect mind cannot produce the idea of perfection

         d) only a perfect Mind can cause my idea of perfection

      3) <u>Aquinas' 5 ways to prove God's Existence</u>

         a) from motion to an unmoved Mover (first 3 ways are cosmological arguments)

         b) from effects to a first uncaused Cause

         c) from contingent beings to a necessary Being

         d) from degrees of perfection to the most perfect Being (moral argument)

         e) from the guidance of the mindless things of nature to the Mind that guides nature (teleological argument; design)

      4) <u>Anselm's 2 ontological arguments</u>

         a) God, by definition, has all perfections; existence is a perfection (the greatest conceivable Being must exist)

         b) a Necessary Being cannot not exist; therefore, a Necessary Being must exist

      5) <u>Paley's watchmaker argument</u> (teleological)

         —design & order in the universe show that an intelligent Designer is needed

      6) <u>Pascal's Wager</u>

         —everything to gain & nothing to lose by wagering on God; nothing to gain & everything to lose by wagering against God

      7) <u>the absurdity of life without God</u> (Solomon)

      8) <u>the moral argument</u> (Kant & Lewis)

      9) <u>Bonaventure's kalam cosmological argument</u>

         —universe had a beginning & needs a Cause

43

B) <u>Arguments for Atheism</u>
    1) <u>the arguments from evil</u>
        a) God created all things; did He create evil?
            (evil is a privation of God's good creation)
        b) if evil, then no all-powerful, all-good God exists
            (God allowed evil for purpose of a greater
            good & He is in process of defeating evil)
    2) <u>contradictory attributes of God</u>
        a) the rock that God cannot lift
        b) is good above God or arbitrary?
    3) <u>the argument from human free will</u> (Sartre)
    4) <u>Kant's agnosticism</u> (we cannot know reality as it is,
        only reality as it appears to us)
    5) <u>verification principle</u> (god-talk is meaningless)
C) <u>Conclusion</u>—it is reasonable that God exists

20) <u>How Can We Talk About God</u>? (Chapter 20)
- A) <u>Introduction</u>
  - 1) <u>equivocal</u>-words applied to God have totally different meanings
  - 2) <u>univocal</u>-words applied to God have totally the same meanings
  - 3) <u>analogical</u>-words applied to God have similar meanings
- B) <u>God-talk is equivocal</u>
  - 1) <u>Plotinus</u> (we can only say what God is not)
    - a) negative God-talk (implies positive knowledge)
    - b) extrinsic analogy-God is called good only because He is the cause of all good (isn't the cause of good itself good?)
  - 2) <u>symbolic language</u>-religious language is purely symbolic; metaphor, parable, mythical (problem-always a literal meaning behind a metaphor)
  - 3) <u>activity language</u>-what God is is unknown; what God does can be known (what God does tells us something about who He is)
- C) <u>univocal God-talk</u>
  - 1) either we have univocal understanding of the words used of God & man, or agnosticism follows
  - 2) problems
    - a) no effect equals its cause
    - b) no creature has the same mode of being as the Creator (we are finite; God is infinite)
  - 3) contribution of this view-if God-talk is to avoid complete agnosticism, there must be a univocal element (otherwise our statements about God are meaningless)
- D) <u>analogous God-talk</u> (Aquinas—the correct view)
  - 1) terms used of God (holy, good, loving, being, etc.) must be defined in the same way (univocal)
  - 2) terms used of God can be applied only in a similar way (analogical predication)
    - a) all limitations must be removed from a term when applying it to God
    - b) God is infinitely good; man is finitely good
  - 3) a basis for analogy exists only if there is an intrinsic causal relationship, not merely an extrinsic one (example—hot water/heat & hardness of boiled egg)

4) the characteristic caused must be essential, not merely accidental to the effect (evil is not essential to humanity)

5) the effect resembles the efficient cause, not necessarily the instrumental cause (exam/pen/student's mind)

6) the key to discern which characteristics apply to God & which do not: positive qualities in the world that are not limited by their nature can be applied without limitation to God (God is holy, good, loving, powerful, etc.; God is not evil, material)

21) <u>The Problem of Evil</u> (Chapter 21)
  A) <u>Illusionism</u> (God exists, but evil is an illusion)
      1) monism, pantheism, Hinduism, Christian Science
      2) contradicts sense perception & common sense, and it
          cannot be consistently lived
  B) <u>Atheism</u> (evil exists, but God does not)
      1) either good is arbitrary or it is above God (God wills
          the good because it is consistent with His own good
          nature; standard isn't above God—God is standard)
      2) an all-good, all-powerful God would destroy evil
          a) unnecessary time limit placed on God
          b) God is in the process of defeating evil
      3) God & evil are logically incompatible (an assumption)
      4) amount of evil in world disproves God (it would take
          infinite wisdom to know how much is too much)
      5) theists use a double standard (God as the Creator is
          sovereign over life)
      6) why did God created a world that would sin?
          (greater good—free will, grace & mercy, love
          enemies, courage)
      7) this is not the best of all possible worlds
          (true, but it is the best way to achieve the best of
          all possible worlds)
      8) why doesn't God save all men?
          (God's sovereignty; human free will)
      9) did God create evil? (no, only its possibility—free will)
  C) <u>Dualism</u> (both good & evil eternally exist in opposition to one
      another)   Mani of Persia founded Manichaeism-200's AD
      1) response—good is a perversion or privation of evil
      2) 2 gods could not be infinite or ultimate (need a Cause)
  D) <u>Finite Godism</u> (a limited god who lacks the power to defeat
      evil on his own)
      1) only an infinite God can guarantee evil's defeat
      2) only an infinite God is worthy of worship
      3) even a finite god needs a cause
  E) <u>Necessitarianism</u> (impossible for God to avoid creating an
      evil world)
      1) God was not free to create
      2) creation flows necessarily from God
      3) a necessary being must necessarily exist (the universe
          would be eternal)
      4) creation must be a free act (an eternal choice to create)

F) <u>Impossibilism</u> (God could not forsee evil)
  1) impossible to foreknow future free choices
  2) response—God is above time; He knows everything in one eternal now

G) <u>Theism</u> (God allows & uses evil for good ends)
  1) God created the possibility for evil (human/angelic free will), not evil itself; evil is a privation or perversion of God's good creation
  2) unnecessary time limit placed on God (God is in the process of defeating evil through work of Christ)
  3) God allows evil for purpose of a greater good (free will, love enemies, courage, grace/mercy, draw people to Himself [deathbed-priest], etc.; Isa 55:8-9)
  4) God's love cannot be forced on His creatures
  5) this is not the greatest possible world (this is the greatest possible way to achieve the greatest possible world)
  6) man's free choice brought evil & human suffering into the world (angelic free will also)
  7) atheists usually deny the existence of evil
  8) the God of the Bible is the only guarantee that evil will be defeated

22) <u>Can We Experience God</u>? (Chapter 22)
- A) religious experience involves an awareness of the Transcendent
  - 1) goes beyong the world of sense experience
  - 2) the ultimate
  - 3) worthy of ultimate commitment (worship)
- B) religious experience is universal to the human race
  - 1) "man is incurably religious" (Geisler & Feinberg)
  - 2) "man is the God-intoxicated ape" (Walter Kauffmann)
- C) no one is really an atheist (even atheists cannot avoid transcendence)
- D) atheists & pantheists merely replace the theistic way of viewing God with other forms of transcendence:
  - 1) transcending backward (rituals of primitive religions look back to man's origin)
  - 2) transcending upward (through mysticism man can reach God—the highest level of reality)
  - 3) transcending outward (we can move to God in any direction; God is beyond our limits)
  - 4) transcending downward (God is in the depth of our being; or, He is the ground of our being)
  - 5) transcending within (within one's being or self)
  - 6) transcending forward (Marx's utopian goal)
  - 7) transcending in a circle (Nietzsche—eternal recurrence)
- E) how religious experience differs from other experiences
  - 1) from moral experiences
    - a) our duty to other men, not our devotion to God
    - b) Kierkegaard—morality deals with our relationship with God's moral laws; religion deals with our relationship with God (the ultimate)
  - 2) from aesthetic experiences (art, beauty, taste, pleasure, feeling; rather than worship)
- F) attacks on the reality of religious experience
  - 1) Feuerbach—a product of human imagination
  - 2) Freud—wish-fulfillment
  - 3) William James & Carl Jung (God is nothing but the subconscious)
- G) the need to examine religious experience
  - 1) the possibility of being deceived
  - 2) different conceptions of the object of religious experience (theism, pantheism, etc.)
  - 3) experience as such does not prove anything other than the fact that one has had that experience

H) proving the reality of religious experience
1) <u>the argument from religious encounter</u>
—many intelligent, self-critical people have had religious experiences; it is unlikely they were all deceived (Jesus, Moses, Abraham, Gandhi, etc.)
2) <u>the argument from religious need</u>
a) all men have a basic need for God (Sartre, Kauffman, Nietzsche, Humanist Manifesto)
b) all basic needs of men are fulfillable/food, water
c) therefore, a God exists who can meet our need for Him

Part Five—What is Good or Right? (Ethics)

23) <u>What is Right?</u> (Chapter 23)
    A) <u>Different Views of the Meaning of Right</u>
        1) might is right—Thrasymachus (the powerful may be evil—Hitler, Stalin, Nero)
        2) morals are mores (one community can't condemn another)
        3) man is the measure—Protagoras (can't call another's actions evil)
        4) human race is right (the world is often wrong—flat earth, geocentric universe, slavery, women as property, etc.)
        5) right is moderation—Aristotle (often the right thing to do is extreme—just war, rescue)
        6) there is no right (we can't live that way; the good is more than feelings)
        7) right is what brings pleasure—Epicureans (not all pain is bad [surgery]; not all pleasure is good [sadism])
        8) right is the greatest good for the human race—Utilitarianism (who decides what is good?; we can't predict the future; good left undefined)
        9) good is what is desired for its own sake (doesn't really define good; we often desire evil)
        10) good is indefinable (no way to distinguish between right & wrong; we can't live that way)
        11) Christian view—good is what God wills (however, He only wills that which is consistent with His good nature)
    B) <u>A Christian View of Right and Wrong</u>
        1) the origin of the right = God's good nature
            —God's will is subject only to His nature
        2) <u>first sphere of God's revelation of the right</u>
            a) natural or general revelation
            b) revealed in nature (our consciences—Rm 2:14-15)
            c) available to all mankind (Mt 7:12)
        3) <u>second sphere of God's revelation of the right</u>
            a) supernatural or special revelation
            b) miraculously revealed in Scripture
            c) available only to those who have access to biblical truths

4) <u>God's absolute moral laws</u>—right for all people at all
    times in all places
5) absolute moral laws—discovered, not created by man
6) the superiority of the Christian ethic
    a) superior source—God
    b) superior manifestation—Jesus, the perfect one
    c) superior declaration—the Bible
    d) superior motivation—the love of Christ
    e) the superior justification—God's Word & future
        judgment
7) the absolute moral law does not give us the ability to
    live up to it (only Jesus can save us & transform us
    from within)

24) <u>How Do We Know What is Right?</u> (Chapter 24)

    A) <u>Justifying What is Meant By Right</u>

        1) <u>Pragmaticism</u> (justification by results)

            a) William James—something is right if it works

            b) whatever brings good results is good

            c) response—whose definition of good?

            d) response—lying, cheating, & killing often work

        2) <u>Immanuel Kant</u> (justification by the self-destructive nature of the contrary) this reduces to pragmaticism

            a) it is self-destructive to will the opposite of what duty demands

            b) if lying were a universal law, there would be no truth; if killing were universally done, there would be no one left to kill

        3) <u>G. E. Moore</u> (justification by intuition)

            —response—people have diffferent ethical intuitions; confuses the source of a belief with its justification

        4) <u>Aquinas</u> (justification by self-evidence)

            a) he held to first principles for all knowledge

            b) first principles are self-evident

            c) response—if self-evident, why do we disagree about morality?

        5) <u>Thomas Hobbes</u> (justification by appeal to human authority; the King declares what is right)

            —response—authorities are often wrong & often disagree; one government can't judge another; God is the ultimate authority

        6) <u>Christianity, Judaism, Islam, & Other Religions</u> (justification by appeal to divine authority)

            a) God determines what is right & what is wrong

            b) <u>voluntarism</u>—good arbitrarily determined by God's will alone

            c) <u>essentialism</u>—good based ultimately on God's nature

    B) <u>A Christian Justification of the Right</u>

        1) <u>Fideism</u>—appeals to faith alone (contradicts Bible)

            —1 Peter 3:15; Isa 1:18; Col 4:5-6; 1 Cor 15:14, 17

        2) <u>Christian Apologetics/Evidences</u>—appeals to reason

            a) good evidence for God's existence (theism)

            b) if God exists miracles are possible

            c) Jesus' resurrection & miracles prove His claims to be God to be true

      d) Jesus, as God, taught the Bible is God's inerrant
           Word (special or supernatural revelation)

      e) therefore, the morality taught in the Bible is true

3) <u>General or Natural Revelation</u> (Romans 2:14-15)
      —creation & conscience

4) <u>justification of general revelation</u>
      a) <u>intuition</u> (knowing something is right without
           evidence; torturing innocent babies is evil)

      b) <u>self-evidence</u> (its truth is evident in itself)

      c) <u>human expectation</u> (our moral views are
           determined not by what we do, but by how
           we expect to be treated by others; Mt 7:12)

25) <u>The Relationship Between Rules & Results</u> (Chapter 25)

    A) <u>Deontological Ethics</u> (the rules determine what is right)

        1) keeping the rule will determine the right results

        2) the right is found either in intuition or divine commands

        3) values are discovered by human intuition, not determined or created by human intuition

        4) the right is usually defended as self-evident (torturing innocent babies is evil)

    B) <u>Teleological Ethics</u> (results determine what is right)

        1) <u>utilitarianism</u>—the long-range consequences determine what is right

        2) <u>Jeremy Bentham</u> (1748-1832) quantitative utilitarian—the right brings the greatest pleasure to the greatest number of people

        3) <u>John Stuart Mill</u> (1806-1873) qualitative utilitarian

            a) intellectual pleasures are greater than bodily pleasures

            b) better to be a dissatisfied man than a satisfied pig

        4) <u>Two Kinds of Utilitarianism</u>

            a) <u>act-utilitarianism</u>—judging each act in terms of its anticipated results

            b) <u>rule-utilitarianism</u>—judging a certain class of actions (prescribed by the rule) by their results

    C) <u>The Proper Relation of Right & Result</u>

        1) <u>critique of a purely utilitarian ethic</u>

            a) only God can be a utilitarian (only He is omniscient; only He infallibly knows long-range results)

            b) there must be some definition of what is right apart from results (otherwise, no way to know if results are good or bad)

        2) <u>assessment</u>

            a) anticipated results should not be used to determine what is right (the end does not justify the means)

            b) God's character determines what is right

            c) we don't usually know long-range results

            d) mercy-killing of deformed persons is not justified (goal of a genetically more perfect world)

e) redistribution of wealth to stop poverty (takes from deserving & gives to undeserving)

3) <u>the right use of results</u>
   a) results of our actions should not be ignored
   b) results can help us determine which ethical rule applies (God determines what is right, but circumstances may help us discover which of God's rules should apply—Rahab the Harlot)
   c) results don't make an act right, but they often manifest what is right (Mt 7:20; right action, in the long run, will bring about good results)
   d) still, good results are no guarantee that the action was right

26) <u>Is the Right Universal</u>? (Chapter 26)
  A) <u>Moral Relativism</u>—there are no moral absolutes
    1) <u>the ancient world</u>
      a) <u>processism</u> (Heraclitus—no man steps in the same river twice; no unchanging absolutes)
      b) <u>hedonism</u> (Epicureans—pleasure is good; pain is evil)
      c) <u>skepticism</u> (suspend judgment on all things)
    2) <u>the middle ages</u>
      a) <u>intentionalism</u> (Peter Aberlard—good intentions = good act; bad intentions = bad act)
      b) <u>voluntarism</u> (William of Ockham—all moral laws are traceable to God's will; arbitrary)
      c) <u>nominalism</u> (Ockham—denied universals; they exist only in the mind & have no actual existence)
    3) <u>the modern era</u>
      a) <u>utilitarianism</u> (Jeremy Bentham—greatest good for greatest number; no absolutes)
      b) <u>existentialism</u> (Kierkegaard—sometimes man's duty to God transcends all ethical bounds; God commanded Abraham to sacrifice Isaac; leap of faith into non-rational realm)
      c) <u>evolutionism</u> (Thomas & Julian Huxley—right is what helps man evolve; wrong is what hinders evolution; the right is relative to the stage of evolution)
    4) <u>contemporary</u>
      a) <u>emotivism</u> (Ayer—ethical statements are merely expressions of our emotions)
      b) <u>subjectivism</u> (Sartre—existentialism; no objective meaning to life, we create our own values, man is absolutely free, existence precedes essence)
      c) <u>situationism</u> (Joseph Fletcher—ethics are relative to the situation; the end justifies the means; love is the only absolute)
    5) <u>total relativism is antinomian</u> (there are no ethical laws) —Friedrich Nietzsche (1844-1900)
      a) God is dead (atheism destroyed belief in God)
      b) all objective values died with Him
      c) we must go beyond good & evil
      d) Nietzsche rejected the soft values of Christianity
      e) he recommended the hard values & the will to power of the supermen

B) <u>The Right is Universal</u>
   1) we all appeal to universal moral law when we make moral judgments (especially when we are wronged)
   2) if morality is relative, we can't condemn Hitler's actions
   3) if morality comes from societies, one society cannot call another society wrong (Nazi Germany)
   4) world consensus is often wrong (slavery, flat earth, etc.)
   5) the moral law must be qualitatively above all men & applicable to all men
   6) if we fight for world progress, we imply the absolute moral law is eternal & unchanging
   7) this argues for an eternal & unchanging absolute moral Lawgiver who exists above all individuals, societies, & any world consensus

C) <u>The Meaning of the Universal</u>
   1) a duty that is binding on all people, at all times, in all places
   2) the universal law can be found in <u>natural revelation</u> (conscience-Rm 2 :14-15) & <u>supernatural revelation</u> (Bible—10 commandments, etc.)

D) <u>Some Qualifications of the Universal Right</u>
   1) a universal right does not always imply a specific course of action should follow from it (thou shalt not kill & self-defense)
   2) moral commands may conflict in a fallen world (Rahab)
   3) the situation never determines what is right for the Christian; God determines what is right. However, the situation can help us see which of God's commands apply

E) <u>Conclusion</u>
   1) universal moral laws are anchored in the unchanging character of God
   2) however, differing situations do help us discover which of God's absolute laws apply

27) <u>Do Moral Duties Ever Conflict?</u> (Chapter 27)
   A) <u>The Third Alternative View</u> (Unqualified Absolutism)
      1) there is always a moral way out of every ethical dilemma (always at least one good alternative)
      2) never lie to save a life; never sin to avoid sinning
      3) trust God to deliver you (1 Cor 10:13)
      4) real dilemmas are due to prior sin on our part
      5) <u>evaluation</u>
         a) third alternatives do often exist (Dan 1)
         b) but not always (Dan 3, 6; refused to submit)
         c) Ex 1; Mt 12:3,4
         d) this view tends towards legalsim (obey law at all costs, even if innocent people die)
         e) lower commands are obeyed while higher ones are ignored (Mt 23:23; 5:9; Jn 19:11)
         f) God commends those who deceived others to save lives (Hb 11:31; Josh 2:5; Ex 1:19)
         g) leave lights on when not home to deceive criminals; killing in self-defense; just war (Gen 14)
   B) <u>The Lesser-Evil View</u> (Conflicting Absolutism)
      1) during moral dilemmas, do the lesser of two evils, & then confess your sin
      2) moral conflicts do exist in a fallen world
      3) moral laws are absolute & can never be disobeyed without sin
      4) the lesser evil is never justifiable, but it is forgiveable
      5) <u>evaluation</u>
         a) it attributes moral guilt for doing something that could not have been avoided
         b) why is it sin to do the greater good?
         c) it implies a moral duty to sin during moral dilemmas
         d) Jesus faced moral dilemmas, yet He was without sin (Hb 4:15; Lk 2:44-45, 49; Mt 12:1-14; Jn 7:21-24)
   C) <u>The Greater-Good View</u> (Graded Absolutism) the true view
      1) during moral dilemmas, we should obey the greater-good (higher law)
      2) we receive an exemption in regards to the lower law (there are no exceptions to absolute laws)
      3) lower laws are overruled by higher laws

4) not situationism (situation doesn't determine what is
    right, God does)
5) not relativism (it doesn't lessen the absoluteness of
    duties)
6) greater-good view is a type of <u>qualified absolutism</u>
7) <u>biblical principles</u> can help us decide which laws are
    higher than others
    a) God comes before persons (Mt 10:37; Ac 5:29)
    b) one's family comes before others (1 Tm 5:8)
    c) persons come before things (Mk 8:36)
8) <u>biblical examples</u>
    a) Rahab the Harlot (Josh 2; Jm 2:25; Hb 11:31)
    b) Hebrew midwives in Egypt (Ex 1:15-22)
    c) submission to government (Rm 13:1-2;
        Ac 5:27-29; Ac 12:1-2)
    d) healing on the Sabbath (Jn 7:23; Mt 12:1-8)

Ethics
(Syllabus)

Instructor: Phil Fernandes
Ph.D. in Philosophy of Religion
(Greenwich University)
M.A. in Religion
(Liberty University)

Textbooks:
1) *Christian Ethics* by Norman L. Geisler (Baker)
2) the student must also read one of the following:
    A) *Abortion: A Rational Look at an Emotional Issue* by R. C. Sproul (NavPress)
    B) *Pro Life Answers to Pro Choice Arguments* by Randy Alcorn (Multnomah)
    C) *Matters of Life And Death* by Francis Beckwith & Norman Geisler (Baker)
    D) *Informed Answers to Gay Rights Questions* by Roger Magnuson (Multnomah)
    E) *Homosexuality: A Biblical View* by Greg Bahnsen (Presbyterian & Reformed)
    F) *Legislating Immorality* by George Grant & Mark A. Horne (Moody)
    G) *A Fighting Chance: The Moral Use of Nuclear Weapons* by Joseph Martino (Ignatius)

Requirements:
1) attend lectures
2) participate in discussions
3) pass 3 written exams
4) type a 10-15 page paper (double-spaced)
5) read 2 textbooks

Purpose of Course: To introduce the student to the field of Christian Ethics (options & issues) so that the student will gain a knowledge of the biblical view pertaining to moral issues and be able to defend that position.

Course Overview (Lecture Topics)

1   Introduction

2   Moral Relativism

3   Abortion

4   Euthanasia & Infanticide

5   Biomedical Issues

6   Sexuality

7   Marriage & Divorce

8   Racism & Ecology

9   Government & Capital Punishment

10   Civil Disobedience & Revolution

11   War & Nuclear Disarmament

12   Freedoms of Speech & Religion

Lecture #1—Introduction

"Ethics deals with what is morally right and wrong" (Geisler, 17)

1) <u>Different Definitions of Ethics</u>
   A) <u>might is right</u>
      1) whoever has the most power s right
      2) refutation—one can be powerful, but evil (Hitler)
   B) <u>morals are mores</u>
      1) the community decides what is right
      2) refutation—one community can't condemn another
         (Nazi Germany)
   C) <u>man is the measure</u> (Protagorus-ancient Greek philosopher)
      1) each person determines what is right for himself
      2) refutation—can't call another's actions wrong (Hitler)
   D) <u>the human race is the basis of right</u>
      1) the human race as a whole decides what is right
      2) the world can be wrong (flat earth, slavery, woman
         as property)
   E) <u>right is moderation</u> (Aristotle)
      1) moderation is often the best course to take
      2) refutation—often the right thing to do is extreme
         (self-defense, war, emergency rescue)
   F) <u>right is what brings pleasure</u> (Epicureans-4th century BC)
      1) hedonism = what brings pleasure is right, what
         brings pain is wrong
      2) refutation—not all pain is bad—surgery, weightlifting
      3) refutation—not all pleasure is good (sadism)
   G) <u>right is the greatest good for the greatest number</u>
      1) Utilitarianism—Jeremy Bentham (1748-1832) &
         John Stuart Mill (1806-1873)
      2) refutation—we must ask, "what is good?"
      3) refutation—we can't accurately predict the future
   H) <u>right is what is desirable for its own sake</u> (Aristotle)
      1) moral value is an end, not a means
         (don't be kind to get rich)
      2) refutation—doesn't really define good
      3) refutation—we often desire what is evil
         (the end is not always good)
   I) <u>right is indefinable</u> (G. E. Moore, 1873-1958)
      —refutation—no way to distinguish right from wrong
   J) <u>good is what God wills</u> (the Christian view)
      —God is the ultimate authority or standard for
         what is good

2) <u>A Christian View of Ethics</u>
    A) <u>based on God's will</u>—God never wills something contrary to
        His good nature
    B) <u>absolute</u>
        1) God's nature does not change (Mal 3:6; 1 Sm 15:29)
        2) moral obligations are always binding everywhere
            on everyone
        3) God may also give temporary commands (Old
            Testament ceremonial laws)
    C) <u>based on God's revelation</u>
        1) natural or general revelation (Rm 2:14-15)
        2) supernatural or special revelation (Micah 6:8; Ex 21)
    D) <u>prescriptive</u>
        1) God *prescribes* what is right (what ought to be)
        2) ethics do not merely *describe* "what is"
    E) <u>deontological</u>
        1) deontological ethics (rule determines what is right)
        2) teleological ethics (results determine what is right)
        3) teleological ethics is pragmatic (whatever works
            is right)

3) <u>The Six Major Ethical Systems</u>
    A) <u>Three Relativistic Systems</u>
        1) <u>Antinomianism</u>
            a) there are no moral laws
            b) lying is neither right nor wrong
        2) <u>Situation Ethics</u> (Joseph Fletcher)
            a) there is only one absolute law (love)
            b) ethics are relative to the situation
            c) lying is sometimes right (situation decides)
        3) <u>Generalism</u>
            a) some general laws, but no absolute ones
            b) lying is generally wrong
    B) <u>Three Absolutist Systems</u>
        1) <u>Unqualified Absolutism</u>
            a) absolute moral laws never conflict
            b) lying is always wrong
        2) <u>Conflicting Absolutism</u> (lesser-evil)
            a) absolute moral laws sometimes conflict
            b) we are obligated to do the lesser evil
            c) lying is forgivable

3) <u>Graded Absolutism</u> (greater-good)
    a) absolute moral laws sometimes conflict
    b) we are obligated to obey the higher law
    c) lying is sometimes right (there are higher laws)
    d) a person who lies to save a life receives an exemption from the law against lying
    e) absolute laws allow no exceptions, but do allow for exemptions
    f) this is the true view
        1) situation never determines what is right
        2) God determines what is right
        3) still, the situation can aid us in determining which of God's laws should be applied
    g) <u>Scriptural support</u>
        1) Rahab (Joshua 2; Jm 2:25; Hb 11:31)
        2) submit to gov't (Rm 13:1-2; Ac 5:29)
        3) healing on Sabbath (Jn 7:23; Mt 12:1-13)
        4) Hebrew midwives in Egypt (Ex 1:15-22)

Lecture #2—Moral Relativism

1) <u>Moral Relativism—Each Person Decides What is Right for Himself</u>
    A) *Friedrich Nietzsche* (1844-1900) German philosopher
        1) since God is dead, traditional values died with Him
        2) soft values of Christianity held back human progress
        3) supermen should create their own values with their
            will-to-power (hard values) Nazi "master race"
        4) without God, there are no universal moral values
    B) *Bertrand Russell* (1872-1970) British philosopher
        1) "outside human desires there is no moral standard"
        2) what if a person desires to kill? (Hitler, Stalin, Nero)
    C) *A. J. Ayer* (1910-1989) moral commands express one's
        subjective feelings
    D) *Jean-Paul Sartre* (1905-1980) French existentialist
        1) no God, no objective meaning to life
        2) man must create his own meaning & values
    E) *Hedonism*—whatever brings the most pleasure is right; if it
        feels good, do it (surgery, weightlifting, etc.)
    F) *Utilitarianism*—the greatest good for the greatest number
        —who decides what the greatest good is?
    G) *Situation Ethics* (Joseph Fletcher)
        1) ethics are relative to the situation
        2) love's decisions are made situationally, not
            prescriptively
        3) Fletcher's love is left undefined
        4) *Christian response* (greater good/graded absolutism)
            a) situation never determines what is right
            b) God determines what is right
            c) still, the situation often helps us to determine
               which of God's laws should be applied
            d) absolute laws—no exceptions, only exemptions

2) <u>Problems with Moral Relativism</u>
    A) an absolute standard must be appealed to in order to make
        moral judgments (Hitler, Stalin) Van Til—borrowed capital
    B) television debate between a Rabbi & a homosexual
    C) we all recognize evil actions when we are wronged
    D) Christ's profound statement (Mt 7:12)

3) The Absolute Moral Law
    A) definition—"*By a universal right is meant a duty that is binding on all men at all times and in all places.*" (Geisler & Feinberg)
    B) the Bible declares God's absolute moral law
    C) man's conscience reveals God's absolute moral law, but this can be suppressed (Rm 2:14-15; Jer 17:9)
    D) the moral law is not above God (nothing is above God)
    E) the moral law is not arbitrary
    F) the moral law flows from God's good nature
    G) God's will is only subject to His own good nature
    H) God is subject to nothing outside Himself
    I) the standard is not above God; God is the standard

4) Argument for the Absolute Moral Law (Rm 2:14-15)
    A) *the moral law doesn't ultimately come from within each individual* (for then we could not condemn the actions of another—Hitler)
    B) *the moral law doesn't ultimately come from each society*
      1) for then one society can't condemn another society
      2) Nazi Germany
    C) *the moral law doesn't ultimately come from a world consensus*
      1) if split, something would be both right & wrong
      2) world consensus is not infallible (flat earth, slavery, women as property)
      3) world consensus & society (only adds men—quantity)
      4) we need a moral law qualitatively above man in order to make moral judgments
    D) *a moral law above man needs a moral Lawgiver above man*
      1) it is not descriptive of what is
      2) it is prescriptive of what should be
      3) the moral law is eternal & unchanging
      4) the moral Lawgiver must be eternal & unchanging

Lecture #3—Abortion

1) <u>Introduction</u>
    A) *Is the unborn human?*
        1) if yes, then shouldn't the unborn's life be protected?
        2) if yes, then over 30 million unborn babies have been murdered since the 1973 Roe vs Wade Supreme Court decision
    B) *Or, is the unborn merely part of the woman's body?*
        —if true, then abortion is similar to having tonsils removed & no crime is committed

2) <u>Refuting Pro-Abortion (Pro-Choice) Arguments</u>
    A) *Abortion is a woman's legal right*
        1) abortion is legal during all 9 months of pregnancy
        2) response—the Supreme Court can be wrong—
            —1857 Dred Scott Supreme Court Decision
                a) slavery allowed/Negroes not US citizens
                b) denied full humanity of Blacks
    B) *Self-consciousness is necessary to being human*
        —response—people aren't self-conscious during dreamless sleep, comas, first 1 1/2 years of life
    C) *the embryo is the extension of the mother*
        1) response—embryos have their own sex from moment of conception (about half are males)
        2) full genetic code from moment of conception
        3) as time passes, embryos become less dependent on their mother
    D) *legalized abortions save lives*
        1) illegal abortions have killed thousands of women
        2) response—Dr. Bernard Nathanson (former pro-abortion leader) admits statistics were exaggerated (only 45 deaths in 1973 according to US Bureau of Vital Statistics)
        3) only 1 out of 10,000 mothers die giving birth
        4) every successful abortion kills at least one child
        5) abortions often injure or kill the mother
    E) *legalized abortions prevent child abuse of unwanted children*
        1) response—murder is the worst form of abuse
        2) 1973-1982 child abuse increased 500% (US Dept. of Health & Human Services)
        3) 91% of abused children were wanted children

F) *deformed unborns should be aborted*
  1) response—Hitler's master race mentality
  2) no handicapped person's organization favors abortion
     as a solution for defeating birth defects
  3) all human beings have the right to life
G) *right to privacy demands right to have an abortion*
  1) response—assumes unborn is not human
  2) no one has the right to privately kill another
  3) it is illegal to privately shoot heroin
H) *abortion must be allowed in cases of rape & incest*
  1) response—we should not punish the unborn child for
     the sin of his or her father
  2) most abortions are for mere convenience (under 3%
     are due to rape & incest)
  3) adoption, if necessary, is a far better option
I) *abortion is strictly a women's rights issue*
  1) response—what about the unborn's rights? (about 1/2
     are women)
  2) abortion does not further the cause of women's rights
     a) a man & a woman have sexual relations
     b) the woman alone goes to have an abortion
     c) abortion frees the man to exploit the woman
        without facing the responsibility for his actions

3) <u>Arguments Against Abortion (The Pro-Life Position)</u>
  A) *Biblical*
    1) unborn babies are called children (blephos = babe)
    2) Lk 1:41—in womb; Lk 2:12, 16—after birth
    3) death penalty for killing unborn (Ex 21:22-25, NIV)
    4) life starts at conception (Ps 51:5)
  B) *Medical* (Geisler & Sproul)
    1) from moment of conception, all genetic information is
       present
    2) testimonies from 1981 Congressional Hearing
       (Geisler—149; Sproul—appendix)
       a) Dr. Micheline M. Matthews Roth
       b) Dr. Jerome LeJeune (genetic expert who
          discovered Down's Syndrome)
       c) Dr. Hymie Gordon
       d) medical/scientific experts witnesses (not all were
          pro-life, but all agreed unborn is human)

3) a new human life begins when a male cell & a female
    cell encounter to produce the next generation
4) conception—the initial stage of human life
5) Dr. Bernard Nathanson
    a) one of the original pro-abortion leaders
    b) had performed thousands of abortions
    c) now recognizes that life begins at conception
    d) he is now pro-life
6) babies who surive blotched abortions
    —were they not human beings when the abortion
      was attempted?
7) abortion leads to infanticide & euthanasia
    a) 1980's—Baby Jane Doe was born with Down's
      Syndrome, Indiana Supreme Court allowed the
      doctor & parents to starve the baby, she died in
      12 days
    b) Francis Crick—won 1962 Nobel Prize in
      physiology & medicine, along with James Watson
      & Maurice Wilkins, for breaking the DNA code.
      Crick stated, "no newborn infant should be
      declared human until it has passed certain tests
      regarding its genetic endowment and that if it
      fails these tests it forfeits the right to live."
      Watson said that the newborn shouldn't be
      declared human until 3 days after birth.
    c) partial birth abortions = infanticide
C) *Constitutional*
    1) Declaration of Independence—all men are created
      equal, unalienable rights (life, liberty, pursuit of
      happiness)
    2) 14th amendment (life, liberty, & property applies to
      all human beings)
D) *Historical*
    1) Code of Hammurabi (18th century BC) prohibited
      even unintentional causing of a miscarriage
    2) Mosaic Law (15th century BC) death penalty for
      causing the death of an unborn baby
    3) Persia (12th century BC) punished women who caused
      themselves to abort
    4) Greek physician Hippocrates—made an oath not to give
      an abortive remedy to any woman

5) Epistle of Barnabas (70-140AD)
6) Augustine (4th century AD)
7) Aquinas (13th century AD)
8) Calvin (16th century AD)
9) English Common Law
10) Early American Law
11) Title 9—RCW (if the mother performs her own
    abortion, she can be charged with manslaughter)

5) <u>What Should Be Done When the Mother's Life is at Stake?</u>
    A) both unborn & mother should be considered human
    B) if doctor cannot save both, which one does he have the best
       chance saving?
    C) fire fighter illustration
       1) a burning building, only time to save one person
       2) he hears screams from 2 different rooms
       3) he must try to save at least one

Lecture # 4
Euthanasia & Infanticide

1) Introduction
  A) Types of Euthanasia ("mercy-killing"/literally "good death")
    1) *Active Euthanasia*
        a) actively taking a life to avoid suffering
        b) active euthanasia is always murder
    2) *Passive Euthanasia*
        a) *Unnatural Passive Euthanasia*
            1) negligent homicide
            2) allowing death by deliberately withholding
               natural means of sustaining life
            3) natural means = food, water, air
            4) person dies of starvation or suffocation
        b) *Natural Passive Euthanasia*
            1) may be morally justified
            2) if disease is irreversible
            3) withhold unnatural life-sustaining
               equipment
            4) person dies of irreversible disease   *Social*
            5) decision to not prolong death   *barter*
            6) decision is not to kill
  B) By Euthanasia We Mean Active & Passive Unnatural
     Euthanasia
        1) both directly cause the person to die
        2) whether by action or by lack of action
        3) the person does not die due to lethal disease or wound
  C) Euthanasia Can Be Voluntary or Involuntary
        1) 1990—Holland legalized voluntary euthanasia
        2) since then over 1,000 involuntary euthanasia deaths
           have occurred there (elderly carry cards)
  D) Euthanasia Can Be Self-Caused or Caused by Another
        1) self-caused = suicide
        2) caused by another = homicide
  E) Infanticide is a Type of Euthanasia
        1) *Infanticide* = the killing of an infant already born
        2) *Watson & Crick* (newborn not human until 3 days old)
        3) *Baby Jane Doe* - born in 1983 with Down's Syndrome
            a) Indiana Supreme Court allowed parents & doctor
               to starve the baby
            b) the baby died after 12 days of starvation

2) <u>Arguments For Euthanasia</u>
    A) everyone has the right to die with dignity
    B) the constitutional right to privacy
    C) it is an act of mercy to the sufferer
    D) it is an act of mercy to the suffering family
    E) it relieves the family of heavy financial stress
    F) it relieves society of a great social burden
    G) we kill animals to relieve their suffering

3) <u>Arguments Against Euthanasia</u>
    A) *Biblical Arguments*
        1) God alone is sovereign over human life (Job 1:21)
        2) God condemns murder (Ex 20:13; Gn 9:6)
        3) man was created in God's image (Gn 1:26-27; 9:6)
        4) no price tag on human life; human life is sacred
            (Mk 8:36; Mt 6:26)
        5) we can learn from our sufferings
            (Jm 1:2-4; Rm 5:3-4; 8:18; 2 Cor 1:3-4)
    B) *Constitutional Arguments*
        1) right to privacy is, at best, only implied & not absolute
        2) no constitutional right to kill (all people have an
            inalienable right to life)
    C) *Other Arguments*
        1) it is not merciful to kill a sufferer
        2) the end does not justify the means
        3) humans are not animals
        4) euthanasia assumes atheistic evolution to be true
        5) euthanasia cheapens the value of human life
        6) euthanasia produces guilt in the family & society

4) <u>Natural Passive Euthanasia</u>
    A) allowing someone to die by natural means is not always
        wrong
    B) withholding unnatural means of sustaining life isn't always
        wrong
    C) we shouldn't prolong death if we can't prolong life
    D) "Keeping a comatose person who has an incurable disease
        alive on a machine when he is irreversibly dying is
        unnecessary." (Geisler, *Ethics*, 168)
    E) <u>Guidelines</u>
        1) disease must be irreversible
        2) the patient, if conscious, has veto power

3) the patient's living will
4) a collective decision (family, pastor, doctors, lawyer, friends, etc.)
5) natural means = food, water, oxygen (cannot withhold)
6) unnatural means = respirator, artificial heart, kidney machine (may withhold)
7) "The dying should be shot with a sedative but not a bullet." (Geisler, *Ethics*, 170)
8) accept treatment that will prolong life, not death
9) we may choose to refuse kidney dialysis or chemotherapy
10) eventually, we will all die (Hb 9:27, unless Jesus returns first)

Lecture #5—Biomedical Issues

1) <u>The Secular Humanist Perspective</u> (playing God) [Geisler, 174]
    A) <u>their doctrines</u> (Humanist Manifestos I & II, 1933 & 1973)
        1) no Creator (Christian view—the Creator exists)
        2) man—evolved animal (CV—man created in God's image)
        3) man is sovereign over life (CV—God is sovereign)
        4) quality of life principle (CV—sanctity of life)
        5) end justifies the means (CV—God's moral law, Mic 6:8)
    B) <u>the humanist position</u>
        1) humans are responsible for the quality of life
        2) individuals have sovereignty over their own lives
        3) our duty to create a superior race/genetic engineering
        4) the end justifies the means
    C) <u>critique of humanist position</u>
        1) quality of life—who decides?
        2) God is sovereign over life (Job 1:21; Gn 9:6)
        3) superior race—who decides? (Hitler, Stalin)
        4) end doesn't justify means (both end & means must be
            justified, God decides what is right & wrong)

2) <u>The New Age Pantheism Position</u>
    A) very similar to humanist position (man plays God)
    B) God is universe; man is God
    C) man spiritually evolving into New Age—recognizing his deity
    D) those who hold back human progress must be weeded out

3) <u>The 2 Views Contrasted</u>: (*Ethics*, Geisler, 179)

<u>Christian View/Serving God</u>	<u>Humanist & New Age View/</u> <u>Playing God</u>
1) voluntary treatment	1) compulsory treatment
2) improving human life	2) creating human life
3) repairing human life	3) recreating human life
4) maintenance of life	4) engineering of life
5) genetic fitness	5) genetic fabrication
6) cooperation with nature	6) control over nature
7) conformity to nature	7) power over nature

4) <u>Refuting the Humanist/New Age View</u>
   A) <u>Fallacies Exposed</u>
      1) what is being done ought to be done (is doesn't equal ought)
      2) if it can be done, it should be done (stealing candy from a baby)
      3) the end justifies the means (stealing a baby to solve infertility, rape)
      4) two wrongs make a right (experimenting with aborted babies)
   B) <u>Christian Principles</u>
      1) God's sovereignty (we don't own ourselves, 1 Cor 6:19)
      2) human dignity (we should respect human life)
      3) sanctity of human life (we're created in God's image)
      4) the mortality of human life (we can't avoid death, Hb 9:27; Ps 90:10)
      5) charity toward human life, love neighbor-Mk 12:30-31
   C) <u>Christian Guidelines</u>
      1) voluntary procedures (should not force cures on others, abortion & fertilization, etc.)
      2) mercifully allowing death (but don't "mercy-kill")
      3) preserve life (but don't prolong death)
      4) never remove natural means of sustaining life, such as food, water, air (regardless of a person's age, health, race, views, etc.)
      5) birth control, but not abortion
      6) correct human life (don't try to create it)

5) <u>Biomedical Issues</u>
   A) <u>organ transplants</u> (should be voluntarily donated, shouldn't hasten death to get a fresh organ)
   B) <u>genetic surgery</u> (should be done to repair life as God meant it to be, not to reconstruct the type of people we want)
   C) <u>sex detection & selection</u> (wrong to abort a child of unwanted sex)
   D) <u>artificial insemination</u> (by the husband is o.k., by a donor is debatable [I think wrong], adoption is best option)
   E) <u>surrogate motherhood</u> (a womb for hire, difficult to give up child, adoption is better)
   F) <u>organ & tissue harvesting</u> (organ transplants from aborted babies is wrong, should be voluntary & after death)

G) <u>cryonics</u> (deep-freezing human bodies at death in hopes of finding a cure, wrong—attempts to avoid death—Hb 9:27)

H) <u>cloning</u> (carbon-copying human beings from a single cell, wrong—playing God)

I) <u>gene-splicing</u> (producing new kinds of life by splicing the genes of one organism into another, wrong—effort to redesign nature)

J) <u>frozen embryos</u> (wrong—life starts at conception, these are tiny human beings)

6) <u>Conclusion</u>

A) Christianity doesn't hold back scientific progress, it sets the moral boundaries for it

B) Christians do not lack compassion for those who suffer, they recognize the sanctity of human life

Lecture #6—Sexuality

1) <u>Secular Humanist & New Age Views on Sexuality</u>
      A) values are autonomous and relative
      B) no sex between consenting adults should be prohibited
      C) contradiction—they resurrect Christian values to condemn
           rape & incest; they absolutize their relative values
      D) debate between Jewish Rabbi and homosexual
      E) some atheists & pantheists are for sex between adults and
           children (NAMBLA)

2) <u>Biblical View of Sexuality</u>
      A) one man, one woman, one lifetime (Mt 19:3-9)
      B) premarital sex is forbidden (Ac 15:20; 1 Cor 6:18) fornication
      C) adultery is forbidden (Ex 20:14; Mt 19:18)
      D) homosexuality is forbidden (Lv 18:22; Rm 1:26-27;
           1 Cor 6:9-11; 1 Tm 1:9-10)
      E) bestiality is forbidden (Lv 18:23)
      F) incest is forbidden (Lv 18:6-18)
      G) rape is forbidden (Dt 22:25-29)
      H) conclusion—all sex outside of monogamous heterosexual
           marriage is forbidden
      I) sexual desires can be sinful (Mt 5:28; 23:25-28; Rm 1:24-27)

3) <u>Refutation of Homosexuality</u>
      A) widespread homosexuality will destroy a nation
           (Lv 18:20-27)
      B) homosexuality is medically unhealthy, unclean, unnatural
           1) fisting (inserting one's fist into another's anus)
           2) rimming & golden showers (oral contact with human
              waste)
           3) sodomy (anal intercourse)
           4) gay bars, multitudes of anonymous partners
           5) over 300 gay related diseases (AIDS, Hepatitis B,
              tuberculosis, parasites, etc.)
           6) not an alternative lifestyle, but a form of
              sadomasochism (L.E. = male/41yoa; female/44yoa)
      C) mutual consent doesn't make it right (shooting heroin,
           drug deals, gun fights, etc.)

D) right to privacy is not absolute (can't privately rape, kill, steal)

E) homosexuals have rights as citizens, not as homosexuals

F) AIDS = public health issue (not civil rights issue)

G) homosexual tendencies are not inherited
   1) it is not genetic, it is a learned behavior
   2) young boys are often recruited
   3) even if inherited, inherited tendencies can be wrong (violence, drug addiction, etc.)
   4) many homosexuals have repented (Metanoia Min.)

H) animal behavior is not normative for humans (we know better)

I) psychological studies—show homosexuals to have an extremely high degree of selfishness, arrogance, desire to abuse or be abused, & a violent temper

J) child molestation cases involve 3 times as many homosexuals as heterosexuals

K) homosexual crimes are among the most violent committed

Lecture #7—Marriage & Divorce

1) Introduction
    A) the family is society's most important unit
    B) one—half of U.S. marriages end in divorce

2) Biblical View of Marriage
    A) between a man & a woman (Gn 1:27-28; 2:24; Mt 19:4-6)
    B) involves a sexual union (Gn 2:24; 1 Cor 7:2-4)
        1) raising children (Gn 1:27-28; Eph 6:4)
        2) union (Gn 2:24)
        3) pleasure (Prov 5:18-19)
    C) involves a covenant (Mal 2:14)
    D) involves companionship (Mal 2:14)
    E) involves 2 people (polygamy is wrong; 1 Cor 7:2; Mt 19:4-6;
        1 Tm 3:2)
    F) involves a lifelong commitment (Mt 19:4-6; Rm 7:2)
    G) marriage is not eternal (Mt 22:30)

3) Christian Views of Divorce (Mal 2:16)
    A) 3 areas of agreement in the Church
        1) divorce is not God's ideal or perfect will
        2) divorce is not permissible for every reason
        3) divorce creates problems (couple, children, friends)
    B) differing views in the Church
        1) no biblical grounds for divorce (no exceptions)
            a) Mk 10:1-9; Lk 6:18
            b) Mt 19:1-9 (considered fornication before
                wedding, during engagement)
        2) adultery—only ground for divorce (Mt 19:1-9; 5:32)
        3) several grounds for divorce
            a) Mt 19:1-9 (adultery)
            b) 1 Cor 7:15 (desertion by nonbeliever)
            c) Eph 5:24; Rm 13:1-2 (greater good?)

4) Christian Views of Remarriage after Divorce
    A) forbidden (Mt 19:1-9)
    B) only if partner was unfaithful—adultery (Mt 19:1-9)
    C) only in cases of adultery or unbeliever desertion & if
        divorcee was innocent party (1 Cor 7:15)

D) if divorcee is repentant (God of a second chance; Jer 31:34)

E) divorced man cannot remarry former wife if she married another man & that marriage ended (Dt 24:1-4)

5) <u>Can a Divorced Man Become a Pastor?</u>

    A) pastor must be husband of one wife (1 Tm 3:2)

    B) literally a "one woman man"

    C) differing views

        1) never divorced

        2) never divorced and remarried

        3) not a bigamist or polygamist

        4) not unfaithful to present spouse

    D) Stanley Ellisen—"God is only concerned with past history so long as it effects present character."

6) <u>Conclusion</u>

    A) divorce always involves sin (a spouse might be innocent)

    B) Jesus came to forgive sin

    C) God is the God of a second chance

    D) how this applies to divorce and remarriage is a controversial issue in the church

Lecture #8—Racism & Ecology

1) <u>Introduction—These are 2 Hotly Debated Issues</u>
   A) <u>Racism</u>—White Arianism, Black Muslims, Anti-Semitism
   B) <u>Ecology</u>—should we pollute, worship, or preserve the earth?

2) <u>Racism</u>
   A) <u>Biblical Refutation</u>
      1) all mankind is related (Acts 17:22-28)
      2) all mankind bears God's image (Gen 1:27-28; 9:6)
      3) all people have sinned (Rm 3:10, 21-23)
      4) all people can be saved (Isa 45:22; Mt 11:28)
      5) God loves all people (Jn 3:16; 2 Pt 3:9)
      6) all believers are equal in Christ (Eph 2:11-18)
   B) <u>Constitutional Refutation</u>
      1) "all men are created equal" (Dec. of Independence)
      2) creation guarantees human equality
      3) evolution implies survival of the fittest (Darwin, Hitler)
      4) reincarnation implies inequality (Hindu caste system,
         New Ager Barbara Marx Hubbard)

3) <u>Ecology</u>
   A) <u>Secular Humanism</u>—we can save this planet without God
      1) universe is eternal, energy is unlimited
      2) technology, education, & redistribution of wealth will
         save this planet
   B) <u>New Age View</u>—we should worship the earth
      1) nature is a living manifestation of God
      2) save the whales, seals, owls, but not unborn babies
   C) <u>Irresponsible View</u>—we should do as we please
      —live for today; don't worry about tomorrow
   D) <u>Biblical View</u>—we should try to preserve the earth
      1) God gave man dominion over the earth (Gn 1:27-28)
      2) man is accountable to God (1 Tm 4:4-5)
      3) we should be faithful stewards over what God has
         entrusted to us (Gn 2:15; 1 Cor 4:2)
      4) our decisions should be based upon true science, not
         political correctness or Marxist ideology
      5) the earth is the Lord's (Job 41:11; Ps 50:12; 104:10-14)
      6) we should rest the land (Ex 23:10-11)

Lecture #9—Government & Capital Punishment

1) The Biblical View of Government
    A) instituted by God (Gn 9:6: Rm 13:1-4)
    B) purpose—to protect human life & keep order
        1) human life is sacred/worth protecting (Gn 1:26-27)
        2) man is sinful/human life needs protecting
            (Rm 3:10, 23; 5:12)
    C) government's power must be limited (sinful human leaders)
    D) God's will for man now
        1) not a one-world government (Gn 11:1-9; Rv 13:3-8)
        2) God doesn't want mankind united in his rebellion
            against Him
        3) separate nations to limit government power (Gn 11)
        4) other ways to limit government power
            1) separation of powers, checks & balances (federal
                & state; 3 branches/Prov 29:2; 11:14:
                Ex 18:25-26; Jer 17:9; Rm 3:10)
            2) God's law above leaders
            3) recognition of God-given inalienable rights
                (life, liberty, pursuit of happiness)
            4) freedom of religion, press, petition, assembly
            5) right to bear arms, freedom to vote
        5) private ownership (Ex 20:15, 17; 2 Thes 3:10;
            Eccl 3:12-13; Gn 1:26-28)
    E) God's future will for man
        1) a one-world gov't ruled by King Jesus (Rv 19:11-16)
        2) the Kingdom of God on earth (Rv 11:15)
        3) Jesus, not mankind, will bring peace (Dn 9:26; Isa 9:6)
    F) Church & Government Contrasted
        1) Church's mission—witness, teach, & charity
            (Mt 28:19-20; Jm 1:27)
        2) Government's mission—God's vengeance (Rm 13:1-7)

2) Capital Punishment (Death Penalty)
    A) deters crime; protects sanctity of human life
        (Gn 9:6; Ex 21:23-25; Rm 13:1-4; Ac 25:11)
    B) justice = punishment must fit the crime

C) he who sheds innocent blood forfeits his own right to life
D) retribution should come quickly (Eccl 8:11)
E) government—eye for an eye (justice)
F) individual Christian (turn other cheek; don't seek revenge; Mt 5:38-48; Rm 12:17-13:4)
G) retribution, not rehabilitation (criminals aren't sick, they're evil by choice)

3) <u>Refutation of Reconstructionism/Theonomy/Dominion Theology</u>
    A) theonomists believe all governments should enforce the entire Mosaic Law (usually exclude ceremonial aspects)
    B) death penalty for various crimes (Geisler, page 200)
    C) <u>theonomy</u>—only laws revoked in NT no longer in effect
    D) <u>dispensationalism</u>—only laws repeated in NT still in effect (law against bestiality not mentioned in NT)
    E) both extremes are incorrect
    F) <u>Refutation of Reconstructionism</u>
      1) Israel—a theocracy (ruled directly by God, Ex 19:1-8)
      2) America & Gentile nations are not theocracies
      3) Mosaic Law given to nation of Israel (Hb 7:11-12)
      4) <u>Christ fulfilled the Law</u> (Rm 6:14; 10:4; Mt 5:17-18; Gal 3:24-25) Jesus obeyed the Law in our place & fulfilled OT prophecies & ceremonial types
      5) <u>Breakdown of Mosaic Law</u>
        a) moral aspects (still apply today)
        b) ceremonial aspects (types, fulfilled by Christ)
        c) civil aspects—punishments for crimes (specific to Israel—nomadic, God's chosen nation)

Lecture #10
Civil Disobedience & Revolution

1) Civil Disobedience (disobeying individual government laws)
    A) God commands us to submit to the government
        —Mk 12:13-17; Rm 13:1-7
    B) God commands us to obey Him (Ex 20:1-17)
    C) when is civil disobedience right? (4 views)
        1) never (we must submit to evil laws of Hitler, etc.)
        2) Schaeffer—when gov't permits evil
        3) Geisler—when gov't commands evil
        4) my view—when a gov't command conflicts with God's
            command, we are to obey God & disobey the gov't
            (graded absolutism—greater good view)
            a) Hebrew midwives in Egypt (Ex 1:15-21)
            b) Rahab the Harlot (Josh 2:1-16)
            c) Shadrach, Meshach, Abednego (Dn 3:13-26)
            d) Daniel (Dn 6:10-23)
            e) the apostles (Ac 5:27-29)
            f) James, son of Zebedee (Ac 12:1-2)
            g) Paul (2 Tm 1:8, 12; 4:6-7)
            h) mark of the beast (Rv 13:16-18; 14:9-11)

2) Revolution—overthrow of a gov't by its citizens (Rm 13:1-4)
    A) Geisler's view —revolution is never justified
        —God gave the sword to gov't, not its citizens
    B) Schaeffer's view—if a gov't becomes tyrannical
    C) my view (greater good—Eph 5:24)
        1) God institutes all human gov't
        2) gov't is to serve a certain purpose (Rm 13:1-4)
        3) if a gov't fails to protect the innocent & punish the evil
            doer, God may choose to raise up a new gov't from
            among the people
        4) just as God cast down the Canaanite gov'ts in the
            Promised Land (Lv 18:20-24)
        5) God instituted one revolution in the Bible
            (2 Chron 22:10-12; 23:11-15)
        6) revolution—only attempted as a last resort
            (self-defense)

Lecture #11—War & Nuclear Disarmament

1) <u>War (Matthew 5:9)</u>
   A) <u>The Options</u>
      1) *Activism* (every war declared by one's gov't is right)
      2) *Pacifism* (war is never right)
      3) *Selectivism* (some wars are just) correct view
   B) <u>Just War Doctrine</u> (Ambrose, Augustine, Aquinas, etc.)
      1) *Just Cause* (sufficient reason to engage in war—
         self-defense, protect innocent life, human rights)
      2) *Competent Authority* (government, not private groups;
         Rm 13:1-4; Gn 14:11-16?)
      3) *Comparative Justice* (your nation must be more just
         than other nation) Mt 7:1-5
      4) *Right Intention* (desire for peace, restraining evil,
         assisting good) Rm 12:18
      5) *Last Resort* (peaceful alternatives exhausted) Rm 12:18
      6) *Probability of Success* (certainty not needed, but don't
         knowingly spill blood in vain) Lk 14:31-32
      7) *Proportionality* (good to be achieved by war must
         outweigh evil that will result by it) Lk 14:31-32
      8) *Discrimination* (military targets, not innocent civilians)
         Prov 6:16-19
   C) a just war might still be fought unjustly
   D) a God-ordained war over-rides just-war criteria
      (Job 1:21; Dt 20:16-18; Josh 10:40)

2) <u>Nuclear Disarmament (Options)</u>
   A) <u>Unilateral Disarmament</u> (Archbishop Raymond Hunthausen)
      1) U.S. should unilaterally disarm itself
      2) this would further the cause of world peace
      3) if we are invaded, we must bear our cross
      4) Bertrand Russell—"better red than dead"
      5) <u>refutation</u>
         a) turning the strongest free nation in the world
            into a wimp doesn't further the cause of
            world peace

        b) the weaker a nation is, the more it invites invasion

        c) dictatorships have killed more people this century than wars

B) <u>Mutually Assured Destruction</u> (Jimmy Carter)

    1) balance of power, both U.S. & Russia would destroy each other if there were nuclear exchanges

    2) cities targeted as a threat

    3) <u>refutation</u>

        a) if bluff fails, suicide or surrender

        b) U.S. values its citizens more than Russia

        c) not a real defense, only a deterrent

C) <u>Nuclear Defense</u> (Ronald Reagen)

    1) preparing to win a nuclear war if necessary

    2) smaller, mobile, & more accurate nuclear weapons

        a) less fall-out (less loss of innocent life)

        b) able to hit strategic military targets (not cities)

        c) mobile—not easy to target in first strike

    3) neutron bomb—if we or our allies are invaded

    4) Star Wars Defense System

        a) a true defense against a nuclear first strike

        b) Robert Jastrow (astronomer with NASA)

            1) *How To Make Nuclear Weapons Obsolete*

            2) 4 tier system (99.8% of warheads would be destroyed)

        c) Joe Martino, *A Fighting Chance: The Moral Use of Nuclear Weapons*

Lecture #12—Freedoms of Speech & Religion

1) The First Amendment

Congress shall make no law respecting an establishment of religion, or prohibiting the free exercise thereof; or abridging the freedom of speech, or of the press; or the right of the people peaceably to assemble, and to petition the Government for a redress of grievances.

2) The Freedom of Speech & Press
    A) American Concept of Freedom
        1) not absolute (can't print counterfeit money, slander)
        2) free to pursue happiness
        3) so long as we don't infringe on another's freedom
    B) Freedom of Speech Issues
        1) pornography
        2) rock & rap music
        3) nudity & violence on television
        4) evangelism & pro-life demonstrations
        5) suppression of teaching Christianity in public schools & universities

3) Freedom of Religion
    A) first amendment taken out of context (freedom from religion/separation of church & state)
    B) public school issues (prayer, Bible clubs, book reports, evolution, 10 commandments, etc.)
    C) Georgetown University—a Catholic school (court ruled they could not discriminate against homosexual students)
    D) public education = unconstitutional (Karl Marx)
    E) public nativity scenes
    F) false idea = religion cannot get involved with politics ("should a U.S. political document, which express belief in God as Creator & bases political doctrines on that belief, be declared unconstitutional?" If yes, then U.S. Constitution would declare Declaration of Independence unconstitutional.)
    G) false idea = gov't shouldn't enforce morality ("thou shalt not kill") whose morality is the question

Ethics Essay Test

The student must answer (in writing) any five of the eighteen questions listed below. Each answer is worth twenty points and should be at least one page in length. This test is open book, open notes, and open Bible.

1) Define and refute moral relativism.

2) Define and refute abortion.

3) Define and refute euthanasia.

4) In reference to their general approaches to biomedical issues, compare and contrast the Christian perspective with both the secular humanistic view and the new age view.

5) Discuss the Christian perspective concerning the individual biomedical issues.

6) Give a scriptural defense of graded absolutism.

7) Give the biblical perspective of homosexuality.

8) What are the different Christian views of marriage and divorce?

9) What is the biblical view of racism?

10) What is the biblical view of ecology?

11) What is the biblical view of human government?

12) What is the biblical view of a one-world human government?

13) What is the biblical view of capital punishment?

14) What does the Bible say about civil disobedience?

15) Discuss the different Christian views of revolution.

16) Discuss the Just-War Criteria.

17) Discuss nuclear disarmament.

18) Discuss the freedoms of religion and speech.